Titanic

CULTURE AND CALAMITY

John Wilson Foster

Belcouver Press

by the same author

Forces and Themes in Ulster Fiction (1974)
Fictions of the Irish Literary Revival (1987)
Colonial Consequences (1991)
The Achievement of Seamus Heaney (1995)
Nature in Ireland (ed., 1997)
Titanic (ed., 1999)
The Age of Titanic (2002)
Recoveries (2002)
Irish Novels 1890–1940 (2008)
Between Shadows (2009)
Pilgrims of the Air (2014)
Titanic: The Sceptre of Power (2016)

First published in Vancouver in 1997 as *The Titanic Complex*
Re-issued in 2016 by Belcouver Press, Portaferry, Northern Ireland

Copyright© 1997, 2016 John Wilson Foster

Cover photograph: bow of RMS *Titanic*, discovered on the sea bed in
1985; courtesy of the NOAA Office of Ocean Exploration/Institute for
Exploration, University of Rhode Island

Typeset by CB editions, London
Printed in England by Imprint Digital, Exeter EX5 5HY

ISBN 978-0-9935607-0-5

In memory of my step-father
Norman Douglas (1909–2010)
born when *Titanic* was in gantry

ACKNOWLEDGEMENTS

I am indebted to the following for their help or encouragement: in Belfast, Kenneth Anderson, Liam Kennedy, Michael McCaughan, Allison Murphy; in Dublin, Dorothea Dawe; in Frankfurt, Bernhard Klein; in London, Patricia Craig and Jeffrey Morgan; in Portland, Maine, Jean Caldwell; in San Jose, California, William Wilson; in Vancouver, Leslie Arnovick, Kathleen Jane Baker, Helen Godolphin, Serge Guilbaut, Stefan Haag, Yashmin Kassam, Christy Leung, Brian McIlroy, Paula Marinescu, Daniel O'Leary, Jonathan Wisenthal; in Washington DC, James Delgado.

Illustrations 1, 2, 3, 6, and 9 (refs. H1555, H1561, H1557, L2620/10, L2699/5) by kind permission of the Ulster Folk & Transport Museum. Photograph of *Britannic's* turbine casing by kind permission of the Trustees of the Ulster Museum.

CONTENTS

'Any fate was titanic . . .'

E. M. Forster, *Howards End* (1910)

Darkness Visible

'April is the cruellest month . . .
Fear death by water . . .'

T. S. Eliot, *The Waste Land* (1922)

T he accidental collision of Royal Mail Steamer *Titanic* with an iceberg at twenty minutes before midnight on the evening of April 14th, 1912 occurred during a night of unusual, almost unnatural quiet in the north Atlantic hardly disturbed by the fleet passage of the ship. 'She seemed to swim in oil, so smooth the sea', a Canadian poet wrote a quarter century later. He imagined her 'joining the mastiff strength with whippet grace'. Reporting Lord Mersey's British inquiry into the disaster, the magazine *Engineering* told its readers that 'The air was absolutely calm and the sea absolutely flat, a condition which Sir Ernest Shackleton said he had only experienced once or twice in twenty years.' On hindsight, it was realized that this calm ironically had made the passage more dangerous, there being no waves to throw cautionary glints off icebergs ahead. The calm must also have lent a benign stage-set surrealism to what passengers late to bed saw before the iceberg loomed. What followed must have composed its own horrific surrealism.

But it was chillingly real in the most literal sense. The

collision shocked into motion an almost three-hour sequence of scenes aboard ship of curiosity, alarm, nervous jocularity, mobilization, reassurance, panic, insouciance (real or assumed), terror, bravery, despair, stoicism. History, especially cultural history as it is today practised, cannot make real that night, nor indeed have many 'creative' treatments since. Only the sympathetic imagination can re-create what happened: many hundreds of unprepared people (once the perilous reality of their situation sank in) consciously preparing to survive or die during an agonizing yet lethally brief period of warning.

Here was enacted with an indifferent simplicity 'the state of manne, and how he is called at uncertayne tymes by death, and when he thinketh least thereon', in the words of John Lydgate. That one was called in company must have helped to muffle at first the sound of death's summoning voice. One's fellow passengers, after all, had the appearance and clamour of a holiday crowd (some in casual dress, some in covered pyjamas and nightdress, some in tuxedos or fashionable dresses, as though – under the circumstances – in fancy dress), except that the vacation had inverted itself and was becoming nightmare. J. Bruce Ismay wore carpet slippers while he impatiently shepherded starboard side passengers into the lifeboats. Casual wear on such occasions is incongruous and unassuring, the intimacy of the living room and bedroom turned inside out: the motley of panic.

Then the possible terrible outcome of what was happening must have intruded: at that point it must have become one of those extraordinary and (perhaps mercifully) unreal episodes when one's own experience fuses with a sense of greater significance, some larger programme beyond humanity that one is being embraced by and that the bookish aboard who survived might have later remembered as allegorical. And as the sinking proceeded, the familiar options, potential and variety of one's life dwindled fast. All became foreground and the present distending moment. The sound of death must have grown clear and less disregardable, the company less reassuring and at last comfortless, even hostile and alien.

When the great ship disappeared, it must have seemed to those in the liferafts and lifeboats that she was faithlessly abandoning them to their own frail devices. (Those in the water were quickly beyond metaphor and even thought, expelled from their previous land lives, creatures now, out of their element, and in the final battle for survival.) The surreally clear night and calm sea must have resembled to the saved in the boats a resort playground in hell, the manly and girlish voices raised not in cheer and sport but in petition and clamour and in the end in abjection and mercifully diminishing terror. Frankly unbearable to me is the thought of those still alive on the ship, borne under the waves, perhaps in pockets of air, departing on that interminable voyage into the abyss.

In those short hours there must have been innumerable acts of compassion, selfishness, courage, failure of nerve. The situation, perhaps even the surrealism of the situation, surely released unfamiliar and surprising strength in some, unfamiliar and surprising weakness in others. Some became people they had not known in a lifetime – changed utterly; some proved to themselves what they had always known they were, good, bad or indifferent as that was. Many survivors must in later years have relived the experience in nightmare, some remembering their behaviour during the sinking with regret, or dubious satisfaction, guilt-edged gratitude, perhaps painful self-reproach.

Like the trenches four years later, this was a breeding-ground for a lifetime's excruciation. There was the recorded self-sacrifice of Mrs Isidor Straus and individual gallantries by officers, but of the scene immediately after the sinking (the sounds of pleas from those in the water becoming 'a continual moan for about an hour'), the American novelist John Updike observes: 'In boat after boat, the women were in no mood to return the life-and-death courtesies extended by the men, nor did any of the crew members in charge – with the energetic exception of Fifth Officer [Harold] Lowe – insist on a rescue mission.' Was there private remorse afterwards or shared remorse and mutual exculpation in letters between survivors? We know that Ismay spent much of his later life in a remote lodge in County Galway, entertaining who knows what thoughts on clear dark nights, visited by who knows what dreams in the small hours of the morning? We know also (from Wyn Craig Wade) that the *Titanic* lookout, Frederick Fleet, was ostracized by surviving senior officers for revealing the lack of binoculars in the ship's crow's nest; that he spent twenty-four years at sea until the Depression forced him to take a job in Harland & Wolff's shipyard; that after retirement he was a street-corner newspaper-seller in Southampton until he hanged himself two weeks after his wife's death: the record, it seems, of a life blighted by one night's astounding event.

We have the testimonies of some but little enough introspection or perceptive interpretation of that 'night to remember' (or never to forget); Jack Thayer's account of the ordeal he underwent at the age of seventeen is one of the most notable survivors' accounts. Girls (like young widows and bereaved sweethearts in the Great War) lived on to become elderly witnesses and moral commentators, celebrities and cherished living links with a time before even the Great War, that uniquely mourned era we call the Edwardian period (flexing our historical dates a little). But in that twilight of public chivalry shame would have been the immediate portion for men (especially first-class men) who survived, and for other survivors that minglement of guilt and relief that is said to attend such good fortune.

What must have passed in after years through the mind of Father Frank Browne, SJ? He sailed on *Titanic* from Southampton to Cherbourg and thence Queenstown (Cobh) where he disembarked by an order of his Provincial Superior in Dublin denying him permission to travel on to New York at the generous expense of an American family. According to Fr E. E. O'Donnell, SJ, Fr Browne was later to joke that it was the only time Holy Obedience had saved a man's life, but surely his must have been a complex set of feelings about his close shave. What Fr Browne did not live to learn was that the great ship broke in two as she slipped under the waves and that the line of severance cut through staterooms A36 (occupied by Thomas Andrews, Harland & Wolff's Chief Designer) and A37, 'the latter belonging for two days to our man Browne', as Fr O'Donnell deadpans. Even so, the priest-photographer's great good luck must have seemed to him and his friends as a small but notable exit in the second act of the extraordinary tragic drama of the sinking.

*

To write about *Titanic* in its human rather than technical sense, without remembering that we are writing because hundreds needlessly lost their lives, is a temptation difficult to resist. And so I have begun this short book with the paragraphs above in case I too forget. But as I have already implied, the experiences of those on board took a collective shape that was universally and historically human. We are all passengers on *Titanic*: this half-conscious realization must surely lie beneath the shallower fan-club, cult-group enthusiasm for the tragedy. She is in one sense that only ship of Philip Larkin's that is seeking us,

> towing at her back
> A huge and birdless silence. In her wake
> No waters breed or break.

But the collective shape of their experiences is also cultural. Besides, it is in the nature of the human case that over time the chronicle of individual pain and loss of life gives way to more general and less personal versions and interpretations of events. And so we are, I think, justified in calling what happened after the collision 'scenes' in a 'tragic drama'. They were recounted by survivors and imagined by those safe on shore, and have since been re-enacted by scores of singers, painters, dancers, composers, writers and film-makers until those short hours of history have become confused with the long hours of the imagination. It has been the fate of those who perished to have become members of a cast of legend, to have died and then in the imagination of following generations to have died and died again. At the time, the novelist Joseph Conrad, writing in his capacity of retired seaman, denied to the occurrence this construction. 'I am not consoled by the false, written-up, Drury Lane aspects of that event, which is neither drama, nor melodrama, nor tragedy, but an exposure of arrogant folly.' Much of the published reaction would have justified his protracted grumble in the pages of *The English Review*: 'the big lettering of the headlines', he remarked sardonically, 'have an incongruously festive air to my eyes, a disagreeable effect of a feverish exploitation of a sensational God-send.' The exploitation continued long after Conrad had died, and has continued to the present day, yet he was wrong in overlooking the recorded heroic acts that were not merely that 'passive suffering' that cannot, as the Irish poet William Butler Yeats, like every other writer knows, constitute tragedy.

Conrad was subliminally determined, it seems, to withhold from the *Titanic* disaster any suggestion that there were those on board who had found themselves in the 'Heart of Darkness', to borrow the title of his celebrated 1902 story. But they had, a claim to which I will return. And Conrad was willing enough to embrace retrospectively as 'brothers' the crew members who worked valiantly to the end and perished with the ship, and to regard as a contemptible calumny the journalistic conjecture that Captain Smith deserted his post by committing suicide. The ringing last sentence of his essay, 'Some Reflexions, Seamanlike and Otherwise, on the Loss of the Titanic' – despite the sting in the tail – belies his previous old sea-dog posture: 'Yes, material may fail, and men, too, may fail sometimes; but more often men, when they are given the chance, will prove themselves truer than steel, that wonderful thin steel from which the sides and the bulkheads of our modem sea-leviathans are made.'

It is nothing short of a fact, despite Conrad, that the catastrophe made an impact not only on lives – in over 1500 cases, a fatal impact – but also on culture. Indeed, the terrible event became itself a cultural addition. There is available a computer print-out of the complete passenger and crew list, with names, addresses, occupations and fate (saved or lost): it is lengthy enough to resemble the cast-list of Dante's great medieval poem, *The Divine Comedy*, itself an abbreviated version of human life's dramatis personae. One peruses the print-out and, following Dante, thinks (in the translation of T. S. Eliot's *The Waste Land*): 'I had not thought death had undone so many.' Like the bookish on board the sinking ship, we see allegory. The tragedy is like some vast admonitory and exemplary work of art, like a portion of the Bible: part human, part divine.

Furthermore, over the decades the event has become a culture in the metaphorically biological sense. It has reproduced itself until we seem to understand how history becomes legend and thence (through the large imprecise gestures of its lessons) in the end mythology. The *Titanic* phenomenon is a case-study in the making of deep culture, human memory at its most significant. Or, more disturbingly, until we seem to understand how nowadays the reality of death and disaster can in the other direction be distorted in representation so often, and represented so variously, that it ceases to be reality and is merely a set of images (either trite or frantically fresh) to be exhibited, bought and sold – history evacuated of its human content for material gain or the prurience of lowbrow imagination. Even the contemporary cultural historian can seem to look with favour on the loss of *Titanic* and its aftermath as a colourful emptiness. 'In the cultural historian's world of "established meanings"', Updike complains, 'there are no facts, just construals, mind-sets recovered from the dust of libraries and tied to stereotyped decades'. As we ponder the remarkable cultural existence of *Titanic*, we must instead endeavour, in the words of E. M. Forster, to 'remember the submerged'.

*

8

The ship's journey to the bottom of the Atlantic was only the beginning of its far longer voyage out and one that is still under way` The astonishing cultural phenomenon of the ship's loss (and recent discovery) is an international one, of which the huge success of Stephen Low's remarkable IMAX Corporation documentary film, *Titanica,* Melissa Jo Peltier's two-part television documentary for the North American A & E channel (*Titanic: Death of a Dream* and *The Legend Lives On*), and the 1996 four-hour television dramatic mini-series *Titanic* (filmed in Canada and produced by the Konigsberg/Sanitsky Company) are the latest – but they will not be the last – fragments of evidence. A Broadway musical will be premiered and a Hollywood motion picture released in 1997.

Even before her loss, *Titanic* was of significance beyond the nation that built her. She was built, Low tells us in his film, 'at the very leading edge of the Industrial Revolution'. *Titanic, Olympic, Majestic, Baltic* and other liners designed and built by Harland & Wolff of Belfast from 1870 (when *Oceanic* was launched) helped to chart an evolution in international shipbuilding at this and other major shipyards. This evolution was partly driven in the first decade of the new century by the competition among Cunard, White Star and German shipping lines. Harland & Wolff ('The Yard', in Belfast parlance), was, however, special in its accomplishment. 'The story of the association between the Belfast builders and the White Star Line', a writer in *Engineering* magazine told readers in 1912, 'practically involves the story of the development of the Atlantic liner'.

Oddly, the international nature of the commercial origins, maiden voyage, passenger list, sinking, and posthumous cultural career of *Titanic* has obscured the locality of its birth.

No North American I have asked (and who has not seen Low's film) has known that *Titanic* was built in Belfast. The vivid and well-known images of the ship and the grim simple image of the city (both before and after the Troubles of the past quarter century) can seem entirely unconnected. There is a well-known photograph taken by the celebrated Ulster photographer and naturalist R. J. Welch; it is of Harland & Wolff workers leaving the yard with the embryo *Titanic* in the Great Gantry in the background. The workers have their backs to the vessel that was advancing shipbuilding technology, and are returning to their homely east Belfast kitchen houses without hot running water, bathrooms or indoor lavatories: the world of Inglis bread, and the *Belfast Telegraph*, which a barefoot boy in the foreground is almost certainly selling.

Can we relate the two parts of this photograph – the

End of shift: Shipyard workers with *Titanic* in gantry

international and the local, the technological and the domestic? At the time, this might not have seemed such a problem. 'The ship was built in Belfast,' J. Bruce Ismay (hapless Managing Director of the White Star Line) told the U.S. Congressional hearing after her loss, 'she was the latest thing in the art of shipbuilding'; it was as if the second fact were synonymous with the first. Since then, the facts seem entirely uncoupled. In this short book I attempt to re-couple them, to bring *Titanic* home, and to do so by relating the two parts of the photograph, the two realities the photograph captures and offers like found montage. And I try to weld the two parts of the scene by reminding myself of the participation by this unique Irish city of Belfast in the great international cultural project of modernity.

Of course, some measure of engaging anomaly will always remain in Welch's photograph, even if we succeed in connecting the photograph's halves. The builders worked feverishly before the ship entered service. Walter Lord in his celebrated book *A Night to Remember* (1955) recounts the anecdote of the masseuse at Southampton readying the Turkish bath on board and finding a half-eaten sandwich (somebody's 'piece', as it would have been called at the time in Belfast) or empty beer-bottle in every nook and cranny. 'The builders were Belfast men', she explained cheerfully, in a statement that is a humorous foil to Ismay's.

But beyond the claim for Belfast's participation in modernity, there is another local significance in *Titanic* that it would be faint-hearted to evade. For many who have grown up in Northern Ireland, especially those who have grown up in Belfast, *Titanic* has always lain on a sunken plain of the psyche. It has been literally and profoundly out of sight (at least until 1985, when we saw the ship again, sea-changed) but never wholly out of mind. For a number of reasons, some of which I broach in this short book, the building and the sinking of the great ship – in 1912, a year fateful for Ulster in other respects – was to the larger portion of the population (those now called the unionist community) a shock administered with seemingly cruel indifference by God, Nature, Chance or Whomever. To the rest of the population (the nationalist community) it was a much more ambiguous affair. Of the meaning of *Titanic* for all the Northern Irish, we can speak virtually of a group complex in the Freudian sense, a half-submerged trouble zone of thought and feeling.

In circumstances I will approach later, we are now trying to raise *Titanic* as a subject for rumination, as salvagers are trying to raise the wreck itself as a subject for commerce. Growing up in Belfast within sight of Harland & Wolff's great gantries and cranes (like mockups of H. G. Wells' 1898 Martians in his *War of the Worlds*), the ship had always been there for me in local legend (as though one had grown up in the same neighbourhood as Cuchulain or Finn MacCumhail), but I did not begin to bring *Titanic* to the surface of my own contemplation until 1993 when I gave an exploratory talk ('Imagining the *Titanic*') at the Sixth John Hewitt International Summer School (Garron Tower, Co. Antrim, Northern Ireland) in July 1993, reprinted in *Returning to Ourselves* (1995), a reprint of the talks edited by Eve Patten. (The title of the volume was a particularly happy one for my own talk.)

Although I did not realize it at the time, my talk was an early adoption of *Titanic* into Cultural Studies. It was thought at the time that the subject of *Titanic* was a very peculiar choice for a conference on Irish Studies. Cultural Studies is an interdisciplinary preoccupation that was then gaining momentum in the North American academy. As well, around the time of my talk, there was a *Titanic* exhibition at the Vancouver Maritime Museum at which I had the privilege of meeting Walter Lord and of having him (with my air of an excited schoolboy) sign a copy of *A Night to Remember*. My Northern Irish engagement with the ship was suddenly entangled in my life in Canada and my unavoidable Canadian engagement with cultural diversity, of which *Titanic* is an astoundingly graphic representative.

Cultural Studies, however, is peculiarly attached to surfaces and denies the depths of culture. Yet it is from the depths that *Titanic* to this day troubles the living stream of human experience. Cultural Studies delights in postmodernism. Its academic enthusiasts relish the profuse imagery of a society technically capable of apparently endless reproductions of itself. But they do not encourage society to have any faith in itself or in any substance behind the imagery. They themselves disbelieve in the reality of the virtues and in the lessons, even in the verifiability, of history. They scoff at the endurance and concentration of power – the power of event, of art, of the man – and are embarrassed by the essence and energy of love and passion: and all of these are components of *Titanic*'s story. It is the dispersals of post-modernity, not the unities of modernism, that interest academic students of culture today.

In the beginning this was a justifiable reaction against the injustices and exploitations of nineteenth-century Western nationalism and colonialism, the hazards and hardships of industrial technology, the inequalities of masculinity and femininity. But healthy reaction has become in the academy a cynical philosophy of surface when it is not a philosophy of power through role reversal.

Then there is the nature of our economy. If modernity was a function of high industrial technology, post-modernity is a function of post-industrialism and a service economy. The 'post-modern' society is increasingly dominated by leisure and tourism, with their image-making and slogan-making advertising, their increasingly insistent attention to surfaces and promissory pleasures. In such a society, culture (a living thing taken for granted) becomes 'heritage', a self-conscious, reproducible, saleable thing. Work has become leisure, liners have become cruise ships. *Titanic* can seem like a casualty of this transformation. The change is the more likely in the multicultural society where diverse representation understandably multiplies. Naturally, form tends to prevail over substance in such circumstances. Better that, some would say, than the old verities, the old ethnic or religious sureties that could, and did, hurt people and divide them. But we seem to be paying a price out of proportion to the debt.

It is no surprise, then, that Ulster too is a participant in post-modernity: the heavy industrial manufacturing that produced *Titanic* and other great ships, as well as other mechanical products of diverse kinds, is a shadow of its former self in the economic and actual landscape of Belfast and the Lagan Valley, as it is in the fellow post-industrial landscapes of Glasgow and Liverpool and the Clyde and Mersey rivers. Yet after some decades of embarrassed obscurity (when even the ship's builders were shy of its mention), the ship exists today in representation in Ulster more profusely than it has ever done. And because Ulster is a place where the old verities have done considerable damage to human flesh and spirit, some have encouraged the post-modern proliferation of images in the hope that the images will pre-empt a more dangerous reality. (Actually, the visual rehabilitation of *Titanic* may be an effect as well as a cause, a sign of changing and more benign times in Northern Ireland.)

But this unmoored image-making ought not to conceal the historical nature of the community which supplied the manpower (and much of the know-how) that brought *Titanic* and other stupendous industrial projects to fruition a hundred years ago and less, a real community behind the images. In the second part of my book, I wish to rescue for the record the local dialect of modernism, the dialect of my childhood in Belfast. That dialect has been drowned out by the Romantic tones of Irish ruralism, behind which sound occasionally the harsher tones of Irish nationalism.

But this dialect was drowned out, too, by a century-old educational curriculum to which I was given access as a scholarship boy when the Butler Education Act came into force in Northern Ireland after 1947 (1944 in Britain). My newly-minted inheritance was Matthew Arnold's mid-Victorian distinction between the sciences and the arts (the Two Cultures, as they came to be called) and his awarding of the palm to the arts. I was educated into a disdain for the scientific culture, especially the applied science culture. It was this culture to which my relatives, particularly on my father's side, belonged. Harland & Wolff, Short Bros & Harland, Musgrave's, Sirocco Works, Mackie's, Workman, Clark – names of Belfast factories that once filled me with a kind of effete dread now, too late, ring in my memory with a sound like metallic and rough-tongued bells, to borrow from Philip Larkin again. My father and uncles did a hard day's work when young, then put themselves through technical and mechanical institutes in a hard day's night. I imagined I was getting a better view of things than they: if

I was, it was their shoulders I stood on to get it. This short book is a gesture of redress and reparation.

To make matters worse, this culture came to be so identified by commentators and partisans with loyalty to the Crown and with Protestantism that I was to dissociate myself from it, lock, stock and barrel, if I were to remain a credible liberal and authentic student of culture, especially of Irish culture. But this absurd and implicit request rested on the error that modernity in Ireland was of an exclusively sectarian manufacture, an error it is past time to rectify.

Communication technology has made post-modernity a more global affair than modernity and can apparently subsist in societies that have never experienced modern industrialism. *Titanic* now enjoys meanings even in such societies; once a Western cultural phenomenon, it is now a global one. Yet it is still possible, just, to see the global aspects of the *Titanic* phenomenon as a cultural complex, to see some kind of pattern in it, and the sinking as a watershed between the cultural achievements of the modern and the cultural commentary of the post-modern.

Such a pattern I try to make in the first part of my book, though given the wealth of evidence I have omitted, the pattern is little more than a blueprint. Titanica is now a glut, hard to rein in, but I try. The cultural significations of the ship, in its making as well as its sinking, and in its posthumous fate – the cynical might say that the ship's death, like Elvis Presley's, was a dynamite career move – compose a ship's manifest of a diversity and compass unique in the annals of maritime history, very nearly in the annals of human disaster.

Nor have the ship and its fate ceased to speak to us from the depths. The English composer Gavin Bryars' revived

1969 work, *The Sinking of the Titanic*, the ghostly sub-aqueous music of which turns sounds into soundings of the dark beneath us, proves the international (perhaps universal) depth-appeal of the ship. The ship lies on the bed of more than the Ulster psyche. That appeal has survived the location of the wreck in 1985 and the bringing of bits of it to the surface. It is one thing to try to understand the appeal, as well as the less apparent denials and repressions the ship has generated, both at international and Northern Irish depths, to take our own cultural soundings, to bring the achievement and the disaster up to the light of day from its decades of darkness and reinvest it with renewed significance. That is an attempt to make darkness visible. To countenance the commercial feeding frenzy among the sharks that attend the ship and its cargo – and their pilot fish, the investors in the 'heritage' industry – surely that is another thing entirely?

Vancouver, 1997

PART I

The Long Journey

But the third went wide and far
Into an unforgiving sea
Under a fire-spilling star,
And it was rigged for a long journey

– Philip Larkin, 'The North Ship'

A Significant Loss

T he international significance of *Titanic* is hard to exaggerate. Not only the building but also the loss of the ship were important episodes in the ways of the sea. The sinking immediately provoked lengthy and pondered articles in such directly interested magazines as *Engineering, The Shipbuilder, The Engineer,* and *International Marine Engineer.* They make exemplary and even fascinating reading today. The American Senate investigation began on April 19th, 1912, four days after the sinking. The editorial of that day's issue of *The Engineer* was already calling for a re-framing of the Merchant Shipping Act that had regulated the number of boats on passenger ships but on the basis of tonnage, not passenger numbers, and had not foreseen ships of *Titanic* dimensions carrying such a huge human cargo. There followed first the American then the British official inquiries, resulting in numerous changes in maritime laws, in ship design, and in transatlantic routes. The first

International Conference on Safety at Sea was convened in 1914 in response to the loss of *Titanic*; thenceforward, safety at sea became an international priority. The International Ice Patrol branch of the United States and British Coast Guards was formed because of the loss of *Titanic*. *Olympic* was quietly recalled by the White Star line and the structural defects of *Titanic* were made good on the sister ship; the third sister, *Britannic*, was half-built only and had the re-designs (including heightened bulkhead dividers and double inner hull-plating) incorporated before her launch. A month after the sinking, an article in *The Engineer* on North Atlantic icebergs called for a more southerly passage for liners: 'The order is, or was, that ships are not to go north of 43 degrees in crossing the 50th meridian, but that is too far north. The *Titanic* was only in 41 degrees 16 minutes, and had just crossed the 50th meridian'. (46 minutes appears to have been the correct longitude.)

Throughout the aftermath, the air was dense with recommendations, the magazines and newspapers thick with reports on shipbuilding standards. Even Joseph Conrad had his recommendations: replace man-handled davits for the lifeboats with mechanical cranes; supply coal-bunkers with water-tight doors; place engines in the lifeboats. Everyone seemed to know a water-tight bulkhead should stretch to the ceiling of the compartment; everyone seemed to know that on a transatlantic liner there should be room in life-boats for all passengers.

Decades later, the sunken ship is still of great use as an international object lesson, a case study, and a scientific opportunity. It has become an incentive to deep-water exploration, exerted some small impact on oceanography, and stimulated the technology of submersibles and underwater video technology, all culminating in Robert Ballard's discovery of the wreck in 1985. With the retrieval of objects and artifacts from the wreck, the ship has become a laboratory for the study of sea-bed corrosion, a field that has grown important since containers of toxic and nuclear waste were dumped into the oceans. In 1986, unexpected peculiarities called 'rusticles' were found on the ship's corpse. Some of these 'rust-icicles' are as long as four metres although it had been previously thought that rust forming at the ship's depth (3.8 kilometres) would grow only at a rate of 0.1 millimetres a year. A Nova Scotian geology professor believes she has identified a steel-eating bacterium responsible for formation of the rusticles.

The sinking itself was one of the greatest disasters in maritime history and still holds that grim distinction. Indeed, it remains an important episode in the history of disasters generally, a catastrophe that sharpened the western world's sense of an ending and darkened the psychology of extinction. Wyn Craig Wade in *The Titanic: End of a Dream* (1979) – on which Melissa Jo Peltier based some of her film documentary – claims that 'in America, the profound reaction to the disaster can be compared only to the aftermath of the assassinations of Lincoln and Kennedy . . . the entire English-speaking world was shaken; and for us, at least, the tragedy can be regarded as a watershed between the nineteenth and twentieth centuries'. He adds, surely with some hyperbole, that not even the wars of the 20th century equalled the *Titanic* disaster in the breadth of its shock or the depth of its pathos, though that the event should invite such hyperbole is itself a measure of its magnitude. Like the assassination of John Kennedy, the death of *Titanic* marked the end of an era of confidence and optimism, of a sense of a new departure; in the ship's case, it was the era of Victorian expansionism, both material and cultural.

The Art of *Titanic*

An extraordinary quantity of literature, fictional and non-fictional alike, has been inspired by the death of *Titanic*: histories, memoirs, novels, short stories, plays, poems. The international industry of books began the year the ship sank. Laurence Beesley, a survivor, published his eye-witness account, *The Loss of the RMS Titanic*, that same year. Before the year was out, Marshall Everett published *Wreck and Sinking of the Titanic*, with a Swedish version the same year: *Berattelsen am Titanic och Dess Forfaliga Undergang*. Logan Marshall's *Sinking of the Titanic and Great Sea Disasters* (1912) established the ship and its fate as the stuff of legend. A brief spate of books followed these early rushes to judgement and print.

After some years of leisurely flow, interest picked up markedly in the mid-nineteen fifties with a couple of American television programmes and Lord's book *A Night to Remember* (followed shortly by the film of the book) which generated the second wave of *Titanic* enthusiasm. From the 1960s interest waned until Robert Ballard's discovery of the wreck in 1985 reopened the sluice gates, with Ballard himself contributing a book and two lengthy *National Geographic* photo-essays. We are now engulfed in the third wave of interest and a second *Titanic* Revival. If the first wave of *Titanic* enthusiasm was motivated by the nearness of the tragedy, by commemoration and inquiry, the second was motivated by the distance of a new generation, one mulling over the values and events of the previous generations that had permitted two hot world wars and a cold world war. The third has been motivated by the technology that enabled the ship's location and that benefited from a widespread interest in space-age accomplishments; this is perhaps diffusing into cultural curiosity and creative sport, and also, on the part of some, into avarice. Sensationalism has attended all three waves of enthusiasm.

The novelists have recently been busy. A novel on the *Titanic* by Tony Aspler appeared in 1989. Arthur C. Clarke described in 1990 his 'latest book, *The Ghost from the Grand Banks*' as one 'which gives a further twist to the *Titanic* legend by telling the story of an attempt to salvage the ship far in the future'; he has almost been overtaken by events in the real here and now. That same year was published *Salme ved Reisens Slutt* by Erik Fosnes Hansen, a Norwegian novelist; it appeared in 1996 in English as *Psalm at Journey's End*. In this painstaking and richly detailed novel, Hansen invents the personnel in *Titanic's* dance band and tells their respective stories which are diversely European and quite independent of the ship. Indeed, the novel's subject is the role of chance in a world in which man has sought order and pattern. The conjunction of the mettlesome individuals of the band on board *Titanic* is a fatal example of such chance. The disparateness of the stories, the fluke of conjunction, is the point. *Titanic* is a chance venue, philosophically unnecessary to the novel, and this strengthens the novel's dispassionate (one might say, translated) tone. This tone lends the events of the novel an oddly appropriate remoteness, an unreality. Yet Hansen knows his ship well and the last few pages, recording the sinking, are strikingly done. Among other things, *Psalm at Journey's End* silently claims the *Titanic* calamity as a European story. The novel is datelined (a trifle pretentiously) Leningrad – Stuttgart – Tversted – Vienna – Anguillara – Rome – Capranica – Oslo.

Since 1990, more novels have appeared: a children's story, *I Was There: On Board the Titanic*, by Shelley Tanaka; *Maiden Voyage* by Cynthia Bass; *SOS Titanic* by the prolific children's author, Eve Bunting; and, most ambitiously, *Every Man for Himself* by the English novelist, Beryl Bainbridge. Bainbridge's cast is the international (i.e. Euro-American) liner set, very different from Hansen's European musicians. 'This place', exclaims the main character, a nephew of J. Pierpont Morgan who has nevertheless served a brief draughtsman's apprenticeship under Thomas Andrews, Harland & Wolff's Chief Designer, 'is chock-a-block with people who went to the same schools, the same universities, attended the same fencing classes, shared the same dancing masters, music teachers, Latin tutors, tennis coaches –'. They are as impoverished in education and morality as they are copious in wealth. Walter Lord had already commented on 'a wonderful intimacy about this little world of the Edwardian rich' that made the voyage for some 'more like a reunion than an ocean passage'.

But the slack imputation of merely idle club men would not explain the accomplishment of many of the wealthy and powerful who were on board. John Jacob Astor, the ship's richest passenger, was an inheritor of astounding wealth and according to Peter Thresh was said to be 'the world's greatest monument to unearned increment'. But Astor was also a successful inventor, a soldier who saw action in the Spanish-American War, and a fearless yachtsman. He even wrote a novel himself, one that shared contemporary writers' fascination with the very technological future that killed him: *A Journey into Other Worlds: A Romance of*

the Future (1894) that went into a third edition. He was seen to bid farewell to his eighteen-year-old bride in her lifeboat (telling her he would see her in the morning) and stand back, tapping a cigarette on his cigarette case. Steven Biel has revealed that Astor (whose family was originally German) was the later hero of a German novel, *Titanensturz: Roman eines Zeitalters* (1937) by Robert Prechtl – the title an echo of the Astor novel that Biel does not mention.

Benjamin Guggenheim, the second richest passenger, was an active mining and smelting magnate, and was reported to have faced certain death bravely, hardly a thing one's wealth would make it easier to do. Indeed, one might think the pull of obligation that financial involvement unavoidably creates would encourage a man to hold on to life a little more tenaciously. Isidor Straus, the third richest passenger, was a self-made businessman and co-purchaser of Macy's: the story of the Straus couple's selfless death is part of the *Titanic* legend. George Widener was a tramway magnate; Charles Hays, the Canadian head of the Grand Trunk Pacific Railroad Companies (and after whom a mountain is named in British Columbia); Major Archibald Butt, President Taft's military aide; Ismay, White Star's Managing Director, and Andrews, a Managing Director of Harland & Wolff's (as well their chief draughtsman, effectively *Titanic's* builder). And hardly lesser fry, including Vice President of the Pennsylvania Railroad (John B. Thayer), a member of the family that published *Harper's Weekly* (Henry Sleeper Harper), London Manager of Vacuum Oil (Howard Case), Manager of the Mercer Automobile Works, Trenton, N.J. (Washington Augustus Roehling, the steel heir).

It is apparently easy for us to derive satisfaction from the idea that such wealthy men were idle men, but this was clearly not the case. Our views on the economic system of the day to one side, under these men work got done, products were made, machinery set in motion, goods transported, investors made happy (or unhappy).

The wreck of *Titanic* – like some fallen giant of the forest – has exhumed itself as a nursery for the creative (and would-be creative) imagination, in particular the urge to fictionalise the historical event. Stories, false and true, poignant and preposterous, have sprouted from the wreck. In dramatic re-livings for the printed page and the screen, passengers and crew have been invented, likewise love affairs and intrigues. Real people on board have been given stories to tell, second (and therefore imaginary) lives to live. These take priority over the real and found stories that came to light.

One such would be the case of Lolo and Louis 'Hoffman', rehearsed for us by Fr O'Donnell. These were the two sons of a rich Frenchman from near Nice who ran off with the family governess and his two children. He hired a car under an assumed name, drove to Cherbourg, changed his name again, to Hoffman, and sailed on *Titanic*. Father Browne became friendly with the children and his photograph of the elder son was printed in the London *Daily Sketch* on April 18th after the boys had become 'the *Titanic* orphans', being saved while the father and his lover were lost. Weeks later, the boys' abandoned mother saw Fr Browne's photograph in a Spanish newspaper and sped to New York, where her boys were about to be adopted by Mrs Benjamin Guggenheim, now a *Titanic* widow.

Then there was Kate Phillips whose story was outlined in a London *Observer* article on August 14th, 1994. Phillips was nineteen and pregnant by her wealthy employer, Henry

Morley, a sweetshop owner who was likewise abandoning his wife and fleeing with a lover. They registered on *Titanic* as Mr and Mrs Marshall (Mrs Kate Marshall is duly listed as saved on Lord's passenger list, but Morley died). Now Ellen Walker, Kate's surviving daughter of the affair, is campaigning to have Henry Morley legally identified as her father and his name put on her birth certificate. Her mother married but Ellen saw her briefly only once a year. Kate suffered mental problems stemming from the shipwreck and treated her daughter harshly, *Observer* readers were told. *Titanic* wrecked lives and sundered couples, but must also have bound strangers together in peculiar friendships in the years after. What other names on the passenger list, one wonders, are aliases and what other affairs of the heart does the list conceal?

The urge to invent, to appropriate and re-shape the catastrophe affects even the historians. Wyn Craig Wade implants narrative re-creations in his text, and Walter Lord's *A Night to Remember* is famous because it tells a story with the pace of a popular novel, with imaginative reconstructions, deft re-creations, surmised dialogue, swiftly established atmosphere, quick character sketches: the 'rattling good story', the 'gripping yarn'.

Of course, such is the complexity of the entire affair – from the size and technical development of the ship through its diverse complement of passengers and crew to the questions posed by the sinking and remaining unanswered – that theories and opinions (mostly forms of fiction) have spilled over fact like sea-water over inadequate bulkheads. Indeed, the whole ship itself has been invented; it has been alleged that she is a *Doppelganger*, a double; what lies on the Atlantic seabed is either her sister the *Olympic* or a counterfeit *Titanic*: a Secret Sharer, if we conscript Conrad's phrase. There are those who thought that the *Olympic* was scuttled during a gigantic insurance fraud, leaving the *Titanic* free to sail for a quarter century under her sister's name.[1] Perhaps behind such wishful conspiracy theorizing is the same intense but perverse love that animates those who believe Elvis Presley is alive and well and those through history who have refused to believe in the death of heroes even when the bodies are produced, Che Guevara and Emilio Zapata being twentieth-century examples. *Titanic* – and we should pause at this – is the stuff of incipient religion, the hunger for association with immortality. At the very least *Titanic* is the power of fiction itself, and the seduction of fiction makes it almost regrettable that the theory of substitution has now been torpedoed by Ballard's location of the wreck.

*

Inevitably, the disaster set the poetasters early to work. The newspapers were flooded with verse elegies, and poets' corners became clearing-houses. Numerous poems were provoked by the death of Astor alone. Within a year, Edwin Drew had published *The Chief Incidents of the 'Titanic' Wreck, Treated in Verse* ('may appeal to those who lost friends in this appalling catastrophe'). Poets of stature too were drawn to the subject. Harriet Monroe, the American

---

1 An odd footnote to this conspiracy theory. E.E. O'Donnell S.J. writes of Fr Browne: 'On stepping aboard the liner, he was handed a plan of the ship in order to help him locate his stateroom, number A37. This plan still exists among his other memorabilia of the voyage. There is a note in Frank's handwriting on the top, pointing out that although the plan is headed *Titanic* this is actually a plan of the sister ship, *Olympic*'. However, the accuracy of Browne's note has been contested.

poet who was to become editor of the celebrated journal, *Poetry*, and to fall under the modernist influence of Ezra Pound, published 'A Requiem' (reprinted by Steven Biel) in the April 21st issue of the *Chicago Tribune* that was without a shred of modernism and was an upbeat hackneyed Victorian hymn to the Union dead who sank with the liner:

> Your fathers, who at Shiloh bled,
> Accept your company . . .

> Daughters of pioneers!
> Heroes freeborn, who chose the best,
> Not tears for you, but cheers!

The most famous poem written in the immediate aftermath was by one of the best poets of the time, Thomas Hardy. If he too was a modern but not a modernist, and wrote a poem that absorbed the shipwreck into an existing late-Victorian (post-Darwinian) pessimistic philosophy of life, Hardy at least had spent years of effort on that philosophy and addressed the disaster with the authority of mature expression. The sentiment of 'The Convergence of the Twain (Lines on the Loss of the *Titanic*)' (1912) is as chilling as the waters that claimed the ship. Hardy's lines give a fresh and alarming joint dimension to the otherwise disparate photographs of the half-built *Titanic* in her gantry and the likely culprit among the North Atlantic icebergs:

> And as the smart ship grew
> In stature, grace and hue,
> In shadowy silent distance grew the Iceberg too.

The ship's 'sinister mate' (like Conrad's Secret Sharer, but a malevolent one) receives the ship and in that instant mating – an icy parody of sexual congress – they together become 'twin halves of one august event'. And now the ship lies out of sight of the human vanity that built her:

> Over the mirrors meant
> To glass the opulent
> The sea-worm crawls – grotesque, slimed, dumb,
>   indifferent.

The philosophy of Hardy's novels and poems is itself like the sinister mate of the Edwardian ambition and achievement he refused to celebrate. The greater the ambition and apparent achievement, the stronger grew the 'Immanent Will' that in 'The Convergence of the Twain' prepared *Titanic's* sinister mate. Hardy made literature out of the idea that we are dogged by the malign spirits of familiars, whose tell-tale interventions we know as unlucky coincidences. The notion of the Double or *Doppelganger* was one by which writers of the late Victorian and Edwardian periods were fascinated, and we find it most famously in R. L. Stevenson's *The Strange Case of Dr Jekyll and Mr Hyde* (1885) but also in Oscar Wilde's *The Picture of Dorian Gray* (1891), H. G. Wells' *The Time Machine* (1895), and the poetry of Edward Thomas (with his figure of 'The Other').

After the sunken ship had settled more firmly on the bed of memory, at least three ambitious long poems of substance were attempted.

The first was the Canadian E. J. Pratt's 'The Titanic' (1935). There was enormous Canadian interest in the maiden voyage and loss of the *Titanic*, in the beginning because there were several notable Canadians on board. First Wireless Operator Phillips (who did not survive) was 'working' Cape Race, Newfoundland when the operator of the nearby *Californian* warned of icebergs, only to be rudely rebuffed. After the collision the Canadian Pacific's *Mt Temple* was one of the responding ships, less than a half day's distance but impeded by the ice-field. The Canadian Allen Line received the first wireless bulletin from the Cape Race Marconi station with news of the collision and forwarded it to their steamship *Virginian,* the third ship to respond to *Titanic*'s distress signals. A message wired from Cape Race via Montreal on April 15th bore the news that the stricken liner with all its passengers safe was being towed to Halifax, Nova Scotia, but this was a cruel error. Instead, graves of *Titanic* victims line St John's Cemetery in that Nova Scotian city.

Pratt's 'The Titanic' is a considerable achievement and, surprisingly, rivals Lord's later prose account in pace and energy. Written in the five-beat lines (pentameters) of English epic poetry, it grants epic scale to the disaster. But this is no airy flight; Pratt has done his homework and knows his ship:

> for the Watch had but to read
> Levels and lights, meter or card or bell
> To find the pressures, temperatures, or tell
> Magnetic North within a binnacle,
> Or gauge the hour of docking . . .

Unsurprisingly, he casts the financiers aboard as responsible agents:

Grey-templed Caesars of the World's Exchange
Swallowed liqueurs and coffee as they sat
Under the Georgian carved mahogany,
Dictating wireless hieroglyphics that
Would on the opening of the Board Rooms rock
The pillared dollars of a railroad stock.

But again, the poem is not mere reflex sentiment. It is eyebrow-raising to read Pratt's acquaintance with the origin and career of the culprit iceberg, 'Calved from a glacier near Godhaven coast'; when it swings south 'Pressure and glacial time had stratified/ The berg to the consistency of flint', causing it to lose its sculpted forms when the Gulf and Polar streams meet, until it reaches 41 degrees latitude, 'its rude/ Corundum form stripped to its Greenland core'.

With great dramatic variety and even suspense, Pratt re-creates the major recorded episodes aboard the doomed liner until the terrible last minutes when

Climbing the ladders, gripping shroud and stay,
Storm-rail, ringbolt or fairlead, every place
That might befriend the clutch of hand or brace
Of foot, the fourteen hundred made their way
To the heights of the aft decks, crowding the inches
Around the docking bridge and cargo winches . . .

then following
The passage of the engines as they tore
From their foundations, taking everything
Clean through the bows from 'midships with a roar
Which drowned all cries upon the deck and shook
The watchers in the boats, the liner took
Her thousand fathoms journey to her grave.

The second significant long poem of the catastrophe was the Irishman Anthony Cronin's 'R.M.S. Titanic' (1931, reprinted in 1966 and 1981) to which I will return later. The third was the German poet Hans Magnus Enzensberger's *The Sinking of the Titanic* (1978).

Pratt's poem is by a modernist poet; in other words he presumes that the *Titanic* catastrophe really did happen, that it was momentous, even epic, and that it both unified with tremendous symbolic force the diverse meanings of contemporary culture and re-lived the age-old epic pattern of human event that, re-created by Pratt, gives his poem its coherence. For Pratt it was the trajectory of tragic *hubris* that *Titanic* described. This is an idea that perhaps was fresher in 1935 among *Titanic* commentators than today. But it was an idea beloved of the nineteenth-century Romantics, who wrote before the modernists, and 'The Titanic' closes with the Romantic re-affirmation of Nature's superior power, the iceberg in the contest 'still the master of the longitudes'. This notion, deriving from the Romantic concept of Nature's sublime and awesome being, still dominates popular conclusions about the fate of *Titanic,* along with the Christian notion of sinful human pride.

Like the contemporary cultural historians of which John Updike complains, Enzensberger by contrast is a post-modernist. Yet like Pratt's, his poem incorporates varieties of sources and documentation into a large structure (it is a book-length poem of thirty-three cantos) – survivors' accounts, wireless messages (canto nineteen lists all the news wires of April 15th, 1912 he could presumably put his hands on – what is called a 'found poem'), recorded conversations among passengers, inquiry excerpts, builders' information, *Titanic* legends. And there is a political structure to the poem, a running analogy between the disaster of 1912, the Russian Revolution of 1917, the start of the Cold War in 1945, and the smaller leftist student revolutions of 1968: Cuba and Germany vie with the North Atlantic as setting. *Titanic* is to bear the weighty cargo of twentieth-century European history, an almost impossible tonnage.

Yet the ship and its cargo are also to become weightless. All in the poem takes place inside an autobiographical envelope: the poem is the story of Enzensberger (or is it a self-imagined 'Enzensberger'?) writing this poem during stays in Havana and Berlin; the poem is datelined *Havana 1969–Berlin 1977*. And this distancing not just of the event but of *the poetry about the event* is the source of the poem's post-modernism. (Political oppression and political revolution elsewhere in Enzensberger's poetry become as problematic as the death of *Titanic*.) *The Sinking of the Titanic* is a 'poem' about '*Titanic*'.

Enzensberger's poem records its own drafting; at one point the 'poet' remembers losing his first draft beginning and now remembers it imperfectly, as we know by turning back to the start of the poem in front of us. ('I fake my own work'.) Where, then, is there such a thing as 'the poem'? The 'poet' becomes a character in his own poem and is even killed off before the poem ends. Where, then, is there such a thing as 'the poet'? The poem diversifies into a multitude of voices and perspectives, and in such circumstances any story, any canard about *Titanic* (such as Captain Smith's suicide or the tennis courts on board) is as good and as serviceable as any 'fact'. Where, then, is there such a thing about *Titanic* as 'the truth'? A narrator says: 'how eloquent are my lies . . . the truth is quite mute'). Words are never the same things as reality – 'Because the moment/ when the word *happy*/ is pronounced/ never is the moment of happiness' – and so words actively falsify. In Enzensberger's poem, narrative coherence, moral coherence and spiritual coherence are all dissipated. Where, then, is the 'meaning' of the disaster?

Indeed, is the event discernible through its own debris and the trumpery and bric-à-brac of its memory? Certainly there are memorable lines in the poem that, though figurative, alarmingly capture some essential force that must have been literally real at the time. The iceberg, for example, is 'An icy fingernail/ scratching at the door and stopping short'. Real power of some sort is going on in the poem and is meant to stand in for the power of the actual disaster. But a disaster with loss of life is an event that thus requires an end, and also with so many deaths a desperately graphic example of an ending. And yet whereas one of Enzensberger's speakers thinks like us of 'end' when he thinks of the sinking, there in fact is 'no end to the end!' Goaded by the *Titanic* memorabilia industry, Enzensberger even satirizes his own post-modernism:

> Relics, souvenirs for the disaster freaks,
> food for collectors lurking at auctions
> and sniffing out attics . . .
>
> Something always remains –
> bottles, planks, deck chairs, crutches,
> splintered mastheads –
> debris left behind,
> a vortex of words,
> cantos, lies, relics –
> breakage, all of it,

dancing and tumbling
after us on the water.

Canto twenty-seven can even contemplate the proposition
that 'There was no such thing as the sinking of the *Titanic*.
It was just a movie, an omen, a hallucination.' But perhaps
the poem implies that we have as much let *Titanic* down as
she did us. For it seems to be political disappointment in
events since the sinking, as much as a scepticism about our
ability to know reality and a disgust with our proliferat-
ing cultural consumerism that inspires such doubt in that
tremendous occurrence in April 1912. Enzensberger, as it
were, absorbs Pratt's poem into his own; in his own poem,
Titanic bears the weight of our belief and our disbelief, our
desire for apocalypse and our fear of it, our fatigue, our
talkative demise, the unbearable lightness of our being.

*

If the poetasters were quickly on the scene of the shipwreck,
so too were the songwriters of Tin Pan Alley, as Michael
McCaughan of the Ulster Folk and Transport Museum has
reminded us in his early 1990s popular public lecture, 'The
Chocolate Mousse *Titanic*'. (His title derives from the des-
sert served at an anniversary *Titanic* banquet in Philadelphia thrown by the American Titanic Historical Society in
1982.) The first commercial song was copyrighted in the
United States ten days after the sinking and sheet music and
gramophone records followed in its wake. Much of the resulting noise was theatrically sentimental. Biel tells us that
in 1912 and 1913 alone, more than a hundred songs were
published!

Titanic immediately entered popular culture, especially of

rip and entered the literature in 1949 with Gene
'The Unsinkable Mrs Brown' (which Biel calls a
ches, tough-gal story) before the 1960 Broadway
mmortalized her.

ould be consulted on the American cultural mean-
Molly Brown both inside and outside the musical.
hem he identifies American resilience and excep-
, with a hint of isolationism. One wonders as a
he hasty Senate inquiry, tinged with Anglophobia,
ilently motivated by an American reaction to the
hat was broadly political to the point of being cul-
powerful Americans see it as failure and therefore
ican? Did they wish to distance or isolate them-
m botchery? Did they wish to seize an opportu-
ply American machismo in contrast to European
(with Ismay as the the luckless embodiment of
, American energetic response alongside European
d dilatoriness?

dsight, we might see the inquiry as that troubling
of American isolationism and interventionism that
ntil 1916 when interventionism in the cause of end-
ean bungling won out. We might also see *Titanic*
that cross-current of history when the heyday of
plutocracy meant the overtaking of European find political power by American. There was tension
American ownership and British management of
other ships, and nationality of ownership itself was
usly layered, company within company. Two sets
s, two main lists of nationals on board, two post-
quiries, two cultures claiming the tragedy: *Titanic*
d sank as an Anglo-American event with all the
nces that aroused.

the remunerative variety. And there it has stayed, the songs
keeping pace with the waves of *Titanic* enthusiasm. To Biel's
busy pages of examples, we might add, as a twig to the bon-
fire, the song by the immensely popular Canadian group,
The Tragically Hip, that was released in 1994: 'Titanic Terrarium'. If the lyrics are to be taken straight, the song appears to be composed by the great-grandson of a Belfast
shipyard welder who worked on *Titanic*: 'he certainly didn't
think that it was unsinkable'. These lines echo others in the
song's earlier part, which refer to an unidentified woman's
great-grandfather who 'saw the future/didn't know nothing
'bout panic,/he certainly probably thought that it was un-
thinkable'. The writer is knowledgeable enough to know the
work order number of the ship when he catches the anxiety
we can feel even at this distance in time:

> There's a trace of mint
> wafting in from the north
> so we don't fuck with the 401
> it's bigger than us or
> larger than we bargained
> I guess it's just not done.

It is mingled in the song with the anxiety that has been
roused in our time by the fate of the planet at our hands:
Titanic is a terrarium – a clever metaphor for the ship – indeed, *the* terrarium, the Earth herself.

The contemporary songs about *Titanic* were mostly
American (Biel has a good time with them) and some of
them were composed not in Tin Pan Alley but rather, as Bob
Dylan might say, 'somewhere down in the Yewnited States'.
Some of them qualify as folksongs and versions can be found

collected in *Southern Folk Ballads* (1987, edited by W. K. McNeil) and *Our Singing Country* (1941, edited by John and Alan Lomax). Indeed, according to McCaughan, the American folklorist D. K. Wilgus carried out an extensive study of the *Titanic* traditional ballad complex and considered that the *Titanic* disaster 'contributed to what seems to be the largest number of songs concerning any disaster, perhaps any event in American history'. The burdens of these songs are not entirely unpredictable: the rich and poor, good and bad died indiscriminately; the rich men got what was coming to them; it was human forgetfulness of God that did the deed; the men were heroes that night; it was human pride that built and sank the ship. Leadbelly's famous song, 'The Titanic (Fare thee, Titanic, Fare thee well)' rang a serious change and will bear a closer listen a little later in my book: white racism, the song charges peculiarly, was the culprit.

There were British songs, too. Two songs released on record in 1912 – 'Stand to Your Post (Women and Children First!)' and 'Be British (Dedicated to the Gallant Crew of the *Titanic*)' – wade in the opportune shallows of chauvinism. Of course, 'Be British!' is what one crewman remembered as Captain Smith's last command before he was lost from sight: the jingoism of the cry evaporates in the extreme context of a sinking British ship in 1912 and the reported exhortation had an understandably powerful impact on the captain's compatriots. The same cry uttered a couple of years later mobilized an army and there may have remained in the call to arms some echo of *Titanic* and her sad captain.

The popular musical response to the disaster was various and could be mildly ambitious. (I leave out of account the five hundred member super-orchestra that staged a vast

memorial concert in aid of th
Hall under the baton of Sir
Musical Sketch (Piano, Cho
soon after the sinking. There
the two-step being the curren
what the steps were meant to
made to avoid accusations of
a recording of *The Wreck of t
Solo, right from the scene w
departure to the pathetic "bi
of the sad disaster which will
world rolls on').

Later, with the legendizing
Titanic entered the world of
Molly Brown (1960) by Willso
a dedicated musical entitled *T
will open in New York City. It
the endemic trivializing tende
al can reform itself to deal wi
moreover, that has curiously s
memory so that mere costume
course, the legendary role of the
repertoire, added to the known
ragtime, lends *Titanic* a ready-r
thing more than that, and som
nostalgia and sentimentality, w
dignify such a musical.

The Willson and Morris mus
a lifeboat more or less comman
Brown, keeping spirits afloat by
bullets. This Denver adventure
become a popular heroine of so

ill-fated
Fowler's
rags-to-
musical
Biel s
ings of
Among
tionali:
result i
was nc
disaste
tural: «
un-An
selves
nity tc
effetei
the lat
fatigu
On
mixtu
brewc
ing E
halti:
Ame:
nanc:
betw:
this a
ambi
of o'
sink:
saile
amb

Conrad was firmly British in his reaction to the American inquiry, despite his contempt for the British Board of Trade: 'why an officer of the British merchant service should answer the questions of any king, emperor, autocrat, or senator of any foreign power (as to an event in which a British ship alone was concerned, and which did not even take place in the territorial waters of that power) passes my understanding'. But Conrad was surely being naive about the international nature of finance and the fact that American money and enterprise were now the chief engine of the ship of capital, a ship that was in process of exceeding in size the ship of state. The deal between Morgan's International Mercantile Marine and White Star in 1902, not to mention the large number of their (well-heeled) nationals on board, gave the United States a substantial say in the matter.

Talk of musicals might remind us that the ship itself could be seen as living performance art. The maiden voyage was a quasi-theatrical event, with many first-class passengers reserving berths for 'historic' reasons (passage on the maiden voyage on the world's largest liner was a notable 'first') or because the necessity of travel could coincide with the publicity value of appearance. The ship had period and theme decor in first-class accommodation: the famous grand staircase was in William and Mary, but the balustrade was Louis XIV; the first-class dining saloon and reception room were Jacobean, the restaurant Louis XVI, the lounge Louis XV (Versailles), the reading and writing room late Georgian, the smoking room early Georgian. Such surplus attention to setting must have established the impression of a floating mixed-period stately home or possibly museum. But it may also have induced the impression of a series of floating stages, with the ship a kind of theatre, in which passengers could not help but sense themselves as actors or characters as well as travellers in the real world. From our perspective, the whole may appear dangerously like early post-modernist *Kitsch* – historic culture literally unmoored from its context, the ship turning that culture into moveable images.

In any case, it has apparently been hard for popular historians not to see the ship's career as drama of some established kind. For some it has been a morality play in which the passengers play stock roles (Rich Man, Socialite, Unsung Hero, Coward, Martyr, Deserter of Post, Stayer at Post, Poor Emigrant, Manifest Hero, etc.) and the lessons are clear, though those lessons have changed drastically between then and now. The sinking has been viewed alternatively as Elizabethan tragedy, with episodes of heroism, comedy, irony and sentimentality, together with the *hubris* of Greek tragedy, in this case overweening wealth and technological overreach (vaingloriousness, Hardy termed it), and a Nemesis of ice – just deserts masquerading as (literally) the cold indifference of Fate – and a final catastrophe (Greek *kata:* down, *strephein:* to turn). Lines from Shelley's sonnet 'Ozymandias' could easily come to mind in their derision of the monumental vanity of pharaohs and other 'kings of kings' and their calling to mind the plain-like seabed on which *Titanic* lies:

> Round the decay
> Of that colossal wreck, boundless and bare
> The lone and level sands stretch far away.

The ship's name derived of course from Greek mythology, and when Zeus defeated the Titans, Zeus hurled them into an abyss. (Hansen has some bright pages on the mythological origin of the names of Harland & Wolff's White Star vessels.) Pratt saw the connection between the events when he identified

> That ancient *hubris* in the dreams of men,
> Which would have slain the cattle of the sun,
> And filched the lightnings from the fist of Zeus.

Now we have on underwater film the pathos of a debris field which resembles the last scene in a Jacobean revenge tragedy, with strewn shoes, crockery, doll's head: left luggage – the lost property of those whose very skeletons have dissolved and vanished.

Perhaps, too, the calamity, softened by distance, exhibits for us what the Irish writer George Moore in his famous novel *Esther Waters* (1894) calls 'the romance of destiny'. *Titanic,* of course, gave a twist both glamorous and dark to what Captain E. G. Diggle identified in the title of his book, *The Romance of a Modern Liner* (1930). But Moore meant something else. In his terms, the catastrophe was an event which on hindsight seemed bound to happen, not just because it *did* happen (like all events, it is the culmination of all that preceded it) but also because our love and fear of what is inescapable – the components of romance – willed it.

Recent living performance inspired by the disaster includes a dance work entitled 'The Titanic Days' by the Canadian choreographer Cornelius Fischer-Credo. ('Titanic Days' has been used as the title track of an album by the singer Kirsty MacColl.) There is also a dance work entitled 'Titanic' by the Belgian company, Plan K, which was successfully staged in 1994 at the Belfast Festival. In 'Titanic', dance *work* is right: the dancers re-enact the human productive energy that created *Titanic*. The music, the set, and the choreography are modernist in their intensity – impressively, a portion of the side of the ship as a back wall implies the entire giant vessel – but this is absorbed within a post-modernist multi-media attack, with film footage and also computer graphics that simulate the iceberg. Hansen has *Titanic*'s manifest including crates of refrigerators – coals to Newcastle! – from Anderson Refrigeration Machinery Company. In one of Plan K's memorable scenes, a flotilla of refrigerators suggests the cargo of machines, but also the icefield, and at length the rocks of fate that destroy *Titanic*.

I have already had occasion to mention *The Sinking of the Titanic* by Gavin Bryars (1969), the multi-media nature of which must have been suggested by the diverse imagery of the ship and its loss, and the complexity of meaning generated over the previous half century. In this work, we are told, Bryars 'borrows a theory from Marconi, the inventor of electromagnetic waves: that sounds never completely die but merely grow fainter and fainter. What if the music of the *Titanic's* band might still be playing 2,500 fathoms under the sea? Using underwater recordings, hymn tunes, morse code messages, recorded reminiscences of survivors and a child's musical box, Bryars' realisation of this theory has become one of the legendary events of twentieth-century musical experimentalism.'

Bryars, who has been called a Romantic and mystic (though his multi-media, overlaid and piecemeal use of material suggests postmodernism), has exchanged the music of the spheres for the music of the ocean depths. In one haunting section of what he called on a recent Canadian Broadcasting Corporation radio interview 'a mysterious collage piece of music', Bryars exploits the fact of there having been a Scottish bagpiper on board by writing what he calls a *'Titanic* lament', a 'pibroch piece' for bass clarinet. We hear a muffled voice, like a drowned survivor giving testimony from beneath the waves, as it were, and the swaying music of the water, and at the section's end the ominous drips as of water that magnify into depth-soundings, the voice now silent or merged into ocean, abyss, the underwater echoes of our fate.

*

The appeal of *Titanic* to the visual imagination is obvious, from the aesthetic attraction of the superior liners of the period (*Titanic* at its launch, at its fitting, at its departure from Southampton on its maiden voyage) to the dramatic seduction of the night-time sinking, lights ablaze in the northern darkness until doused at the end, the dramatic forward plunge like a diver who has hesitated long enough, the vessel stern high until vertical, tiny figures abandoning ship, lifeboat spectators in the foreground, aghast and helpless.

And so there have been innumerable paintings, begun almost immediately with Max Beckmann's large expressionist canvas, 'The Sinking of the *Titanic*'. Harley Crossley, Harry J. Janson, and Ken Marschall are among the recent artists who have turned portraiture of *Titanic* (launch, passage, sinking) into a popular, middlebrow kind of genre painting. Marschall's have a scientific particularity and he has become the equivalent of the artist who accompanies the naturalist expedition or, indeed, the artist who goes to war (he was a member of Ballard's search for *Titanic*'s sister ship, *Britannic*).

There have also been countless reels of films, documentary and dramatic alike, with documentaries and 'docu-dramas' gaining ground since Ballard's discovery of the wreck, as visual recording technology advances, as historical research progresses, and as our threshold for fictional realism heightens. We live in age of hunger for facts and information, perhaps at the expense of simple narratives that express those values we once called verities; we devour histories, biographies, autobiographies, 'fact-based' stories.

The most famous film of the disaster is the 1958 British movie of the 1955 book by Lord, *A Night to Remember*, adapted for the screen by the thriller-writer Eric Ambler and produced by a remarkable Belfastman, William MacQuitty. Lord's book itself was preceded, Biel tells us, by a CBS television documentary in 1955 and followed in 1956 by a live NBC dramatised version of the book. Neither Lord's book nor the 1958 film would be to today's taste and have now become important period pieces. The heroism and chivalry they register amidst their realism, their sense of an ending for older values, must have appealed to both America and Britain, particularly Britain as she faced the end of her empire, with the Suez fiasco a year away when Lord's book came out and two years before the movie came out. The loss of *Titanic* could read subliminally like an Edwardian premonition of Britain's sunken prestige, her dashed hopes for continued greatness.

Yet both book and film were defining moments in American popular knowledge of and fascination with *Titanic*. Beside the 1958 film, the earlier Hollywood movie, *Titanic* (1953), starring Clifton Webb and Barbara Stanwyck, is a poor effort, outstripped artistically and commercially by the British movie. In 1979 appeared *S.O.S. Titanic*, a made-for-television movie directed by William Hale and starring David Janssen (the Fugitive) and turning the 1953 and 1958 movies into 'docu-drama'. I have seen a poster for a 1980 movie, *Search for the Titanic*, starring Orson Welles, but can discover only the record of a television documentary on Jack Grimm's failed search for the wreck that same year, narrated by Welles. In 1980 there was a mediocre Hollywood movie, *Raise the Titanic*, directed by Jerry Jameson, which combines space-age technophilia with space-race Russophobia. This began life as a best-selling 1976 novel before becoming a comic strip in 1977. Biel has interesting pages on the American films and their American cultural meanings; the Jameson film and the Clive Cussler novel it sprang from belong firmly to the Cold War and involve a fictitious cargo sunk with *Titanic*: a fictitious mineral, byzanium, of vital use to the Pentagon. (The Russians are coming, the Russians are coming – to salvage *Titanic*!)

Titanic, indeed, is in danger of becoming a studio character, a moveable beast like King Kong, a moveable feast for film-makers who can create new situations and cast of characters around her, writing new stories for new decades. Unsurprisingly, there has been a horror film set on board the ship, made by the celebrated Hammer Film Productions. James Cameron, director of *The Abyss*, is as I write making *Titanic,* a multi-million dollar 'epic'. The lure of the subject may now be entertainment-industry titanism, the megaproject which can tempt the artist by technological capability into grandiosity, a shallow *hubris*.

A fascinating cinematic chapter is supplied by Germany, several of whose movie-makers showed great interest in *Titanic*. In 1955, the German director Herbert Selpin's 1943 film *Titanic* was released because the 1953 Hollywood film had, as it were, pre-empted the propaganda value of Selpin's work. Although it was premiered in occupied Paris in November 1943, Selpin's film was banned in Germany by the Nazis because it was deemed insufficiently anti-British, because it depicted scenes of panic (which were thought hazardous to German war morale), and because Selpin had come to the attention of the Gestapo. He had crossed the German officers who disrupted filming of *Titanic,* was arrested, and was 'found' dead in his cell in July 1942 (after filming was completed but the editing unfinished) in what was said officially to be a case of suicide but was almost certainly a case of official murder. Meanwhile Goebbels had circulated an indictment of the director around the German film industry *pour encourager les autres.*

Britain objected to release of the film by the German Film Board in 1949 and in March 1950 it was banned in West Germany and Allied Berlin, but the Soviets happily showed it in East Germany and Communist Berlin. From the bottom of the ocean, *Titanic* managed to infiltrate the Second World War and then the Cold War! Something of a bone of contention between Britain and the United States when it sank, *Titanic* became in Selpin's imagination a symbolic site of struggle between Germany and Britain before it became such a site (in Cussler's imagination) for the struggle between America and the Soviet Union. Only when Hollywood took the sting from the film by making its own *Titanic*, did Selpin's movie see the uninterrupted light of day (or darkness of the theatre).

One can see why the British were more offended by Selpin's film than the Americans. Astor and Ismay are the villains, specimens of Anglo-American capitalism in its worst guise – inhuman, greedy, self-serving. But John Jacob and his bride become Lord and Lady Astor and Ismay by turns Sir Bruce Ismay and Lord Ismay: both, in other words, embody effete

British aristocratic corruption. Their actions are dictated solely by stock market concerns; passage across the Atlantic in record time is meant to boost falling White Star stock value. First class is a nest of corruption, with bribery and insider trading rampant; since time is money, the ship is made to sail at maximum knots with the inevitable result. (The implicit contrast is between capitalism and national socialism.) Captain Smith is bribed but at last learns the error of his ways. He had refused to listen to the iceberg warnings of First Officer Petersen (invented by Selpin but he rounds on Ismay as Fifth Officer Lowe rounded upon him during the loading of the lifeboats), the hero of the film.

Indeed, the movie clearly distinguishes officers from capitalist passengers and pits the officer class, with its code of conduct, against the financier class with its striving individuals devoid of loyalty and allegiance. Petersen permits Ismay a place in a lifeboat so that he can be held responsible later. (Selpin ignores the fate of Astor, presumably because Astor's fortitude would have muddied the icy waters of propaganda.) In a sentiment curiously reminiscent of Conrad's reaction to the disaster, Petersen denounces the new seamanship, one dictated by commercial rather than marine interests.

Much of this should have pleased the Nazis. The whole film has a naval feel to it, reflecting the wartime in which it was made. The band even plays martial music before Selpin relents and has them play, but perfunctorily, 'Nearer My God to Thee'. The iceberg, one gets the impression, does the job that the Nazis a quarter century later felt the officers (for which read, Nazi troopers) would themselves have to do: drive the traders from the Nazi temple.

Perhaps Nazi reaction to the film was personally directed at the truculent Selpin, and reasons for prohibiting the film drummed up. For the scenes of panic are unavoidable, and Selpin even depicts a steerage couple who stay calm and dignified throughout the ordeal and who clearly represent good sturdy German *volk*. And the film portrays British venality to the point of caricature. But perhaps the Nazis sensed that Selpin in his film had become interested in the disaster in a way that transcended politics, that this incipiently fine film had perversely insisted on depicting the human and not just the Anglo-American inhuman dimension of the event, had insisted on depicting a tragedy and not just an economic foregone conclusion, which was not what the Nazis meant at all.

To turn from dramatic features to documentaries is to turn from models and mock-ups of *Titanic* of varying convincingness to photographs, plans and eventually actual underwater footage of the real thing. (Selpin used an obvious model for distance shots of the ship at sea, but makes up for this with the studied opulence of his interiors.) Stephen Low's film *Titanica* must be among the most striking of the numerous documentaries. Astounding views of the sunken ship punctuate a partially re-created story of an American-Russian expedition. The film has the distinctive IMAX surround effect and is projected on a screen four storeys high; it is a hi-tech movie saluting its own technology as well as the technologies both of deep-water exploration and of the *Titanic,* a celebration of the fraternity of cutting-edge applied science. Charles Pellegrino is an enthusiastic member of this fraternity, as his book, *Her Name, Titanic* (1988), demonstrates in its splicing of *Titanic*'s technology with the technology of Ballard's search for the vessel.

A different kind of celebration is the film recently released on video which is about the making of the movie, *A Night to Remember,* an example of the fertile reproduction of *Titanic* representations; films and books about *Titanic* have now themselves become the subject-matter for further films and books. The art of *Titanic* is truly a cultural industry: the ship has become her fanatical admirers.

Television, meanwhile, has capitalized on the unanswered questions raised by *Titanic* and many of the document-aries have been investigatory in approach. One reason for the continued fascination with *Titanic* is that it enjoys the permanent status of Unsolved Case, and new questions are posed as old ones are answered. An almost random example of such a television programme would be the 1983 Tele-vision South film, *A Question of Murder,* distributed as a video in North America by Mary Tyler Moore Enterprises Inc. The title derives from a recorded remark by a surviving crew member, Frank Prentice, to the effect that in the light of the inadequate number of lifeboats, the loss of life was a kind of murder. The programme alleges that Alexander Carlisle, a Harland & Wolff designer, forwarded plans to the White Star Line's Ismay and Harold Sanderson for extra lifeboats but that the plans were ignored. Missing British Board of Trade files and a blueprint discovered after White Star merged with Cunard in 1934 make The Lifeboat Ques-tion one of the intriguing components of the case, alongside, among others, The Speed Question, The Shipboard Fire Question, The Confined Steerage Passengers Question, The Mystery Ship Question, and, on a lesser note, The Last Song to be Played Question.

*

Not only has *Titanic* inspired art (on many occasions 'inspired' is far too grand a word), but the ship carried culture in her cargo and her passenger list. A valuable copy of the *Rubayait of Omar Khayyam* was said to have accompanied the ship to the bottom, and a 1598 edition of the essays of Francis Bacon. It has also been said that the ship carried an Egyptian royal mummy, a 4000 year-old priestess of Thebes. The serial movie star Dorothy Gibson was aboard and was saved – indeed, she starred in a movie released a *month* after the sinking, according to Biel: *Saved from the Titanic*. Also on board was Henry B. Harris, a Broadway producer (his wife made it but he did not). W. T. Stead, the celebrated British editor and spiritualist, did not survive, though posthumously he dictated his account of his drowning and 'passing over' to a medium (*The Blue Island*, 1922). Nor did Frank Millet, the American painter, survive, though Paul Chevre, the sculptor, did. Jacques Futrelle the mystery writer lost his life, but Mrs Helen Churchill Candee, author of *How Women May Earn a Living* (1900) and *An Oklahoma Romance* (1901), survived to enjoy the publication in 1912 of *The Tapestry Book* and *Angkor the Magnificent* (1924) and *New Journeys in Old Asia* (1927). It was Candee who related the since celebrated story of Mrs Isidor Straus' refusal to leave her husband on board the doomed liner, choosing almost certain death instead: a *Titanic* romance that has been filled out, using fictional characters, by the best-selling novelist Danielle Steel and numerous script-writers.

The names of Guggenheim and Widener among the lost passengers also lead us, by memorial and bequest, into the world of culture, intellect and the academy. Eleanor Widener, who lost her husband, gave Harvard University two million dollars for a new library in memory of her son Harry whom she also lost (with the Bacon essays in his pocket).

The name Guggenheim is familiar to every academic and artist in the United States who seeks a prestigious grant for research. J. Pierpont Morgan was head of International Mercantile Marine, which effectively owned the White Star Line. He came to Belfast for the launch of *Titanic* (on which he had his own reserved state room) but by good fortune did not travel on the maiden voyage. He was, of course, founder of the famous J. Pierpont Morgan Library in New York City which grew out of Morgan's opulent collections of books and manuscripts. In the previous century, John Jacob Astor's ancestor had left the Astor Library to New York City where it became the New York Public Library.

Because of the extent of its international population cross-section, *Titanic* was an extraordinary cultural microcosm. Lord writes that his book 'is really about the last night of a small town', but culturally it was more like a metropolis. Astonishingly, and with some irony, the ship's debris is scattered over an area the size of London. Town, city, metropolis, theatre: the sunken ship has also been called – with a lapse of historical sense – a 'haunted Victorian mansion': the metaphors, like the representations, proliferate.

Panic and Emptiness

So, too, do the meanings. *Titanic* and its foundering quickly accumulated meanings in the popular mind that had currency far beyond Britain and long after the decade that ought to have dwarfed them with the awesome events of the Great War. Even so, the ship immediately became symbolic proof of the unique inequality of British society, even though many of the wealthy aboard were American. (Indeed, the first-class passengers, tuxedoed or evening-dressed, sipping cocktails, listening to ragtime, seem to anticipate the world of F. Scott Fitzgerald.)

The physical lay-out of the ship both in plan and in reality was like a blueprint of the British class system. The vertical system of decks and the vertical system of social stratification seemed related; the first seemed to put into blatant architectural form the familiar spatial metaphors of 'the lower orders' and 'the upper classes'. The distinctions were highly considered: third-class toilet bowls were iron, second-class porcelain, first-class marble. The bulkhead system, technically advanced but ultimately unequal to the task of keeping the ship afloat, is another suggestive metaphor of segregation. The passenger class structure was duplicated, though in a more complicated way, in a crew hierarchy that included captain, officers, engineers, lesser deck crew, victualling crew, and firemen and stokers, the hierarchy answering roughly a vertical system of decks (life below decks recalling life below stairs in mansions). In received wisdom it was the Great War that exposed, and showed to be inefficient at times of crisis, the more infamous aspects of the British class system, but their lethal absurdity had already been revealed by the events of April 14th–15th, 1912.

Despite the presence of other classes on board, the ship could be said to have represented one of those 'islands of money' that E. M. Forster has his heroines, the Schlegel sisters, guiltily inhabit in *Howards End*, a novel published in 1910 and full of intimations of disaster that the *Titanic* tragedy fulfilled. 'Remember the submerged', Forster cautions us, and when we consider the proportion of third class passengers who perished, Forster's image of impoverishment as a kind of drowning seems like a prophecy.

While registering the malignity of the British class system

demonstrated on board, it is only honest to recognize that our attitude to The Class Question that was posed by *Titanic* is not without hypocrisy. I wonder if we haven't tried to make the ship a kind of scapegoat, bearing to the bottom our own unease about wealth and position. North Americans who find the old three-class division on British ships and trains especially absurd make no objection to the identical division on modern passenger planes on which attempts are made to restrict movement between cabins. Perhaps this is because the second and third classes are thinly disguised respectively as 'business', 'executive' or 'club' class and as 'world traveller', 'hospitality' or 'coach' class or some such euphemisms. (The word 'class' is retained only in the term 'first class' where it is unequivocally an honorific.) Nor have I ever seen an airline passenger refuse upgrading or complain about the improved treatment he or she received as a result – more comfortable seating, better food and wine, more deference on the part of cabin staff, earlier boarding, earlier de-planing.

If anything, the Victorians and Edwardians were more honest about social divisions. Of course, the connection between economic wealth and social class has since been weakened, and likewise the connection between social class and breeding or pedigree. But then, most of the wealthy on board *Titanic* lived in a society that was in process of weakening these very connections. Some of the wealthy were actually pioneer practitioners of the so-called 'American Dream' (which in fact is a very practical and un-dreamy affair) and precursors of post-Great War British society in which aristocracy played a shrunken role. Ironically, the self-made men on board, the New Rich, have over the decades come in for rougher handling by commentators 'liberated' from social class than the lords and ladies.

A more serious indictment of Edwardian society is that it was mostly uncaring about those who sank below the poverty level, who hardly registered at the bottom end of the social scale, who fell out of sight into Forster's 'abyss'. Those commentators who savagely attack the class system on board *Titanic* are the same who show almost no detailed interest in the lives and fates of the steerage passengers but are drawn to the wealthy and cultured on board.

I have already implied that the record of heroism – or at least stoicism and self-possession – during the last hours of the ship does not have a simple relationship to social status. The matter is complicated by the fact that commentators – like the artists – have shown a disproportionate interest in the first-class passengers. This is because more information is available on those passengers, in some cases because the passengers were known before they walked up the gangplank. The full record of quiet heroism, of large self-sacrificing acts, of small acts of unsolicited altruism, will never be known, and it is possible that among second-class and third-class passengers there were gestures and re-actions as noble as those recorded among some first-class fellow travellers. Almost certainly there were unrecorded acts of bravery among the deck crew and engineers. But that some first-class men behaved with commendable *sang-froid* amounting to heroism in the face of imminent death by drowning is beyond doubt. Whereas 42 per cent of third-class women and children were rescued, only 32 per cent of first-class men made it to New York; a far higher percentage of the third-class women and children ought to have been saved, but at least two-thirds of the first-class men accepted the women-and-children first code.

Of course, the power of *noblesse oblige* seems to have

been so strong as late as 1912 that the heroism we speak of could be regarded as belonging more to the system than to the individual. If I suspect that heroism had nevertheless become acutely problematical by 1912 and that events on board *Titanic* and her lifeboats focused the issue remarkably, it is partly because Forster had devoted an important plot-strand of *Howards End* to the subject. This novel was published two years before the disaster and while *Olympic* and *Titanic* were raising their heroic forms in Belfast. Forster associates traditional heroism with martialism and economic imperialism and it is of course male. He undermines its triumphalism with 'the goblin footfall', the mischief of fate that triggers 'panic and emptiness'. Forster wants a quieter, one might say bi-sexual heroism, and because the Heroism Question is linked with the Class Question, he rejects a hereditary aristocracy for an aristocracy of the plucky and sensitive. This is exemplary, but in moments of great hazard it may be that a fortifying traditional expectation of practical altruism and a code for its orderly expression is a welcome auxiliary to pluck and sensitivity.

Conrad in *Heart of Darkness* had already tried to show the horrifying empty heroism of the imperialist adventurer, so ten years later when *Titanic* went down amongst claims of heroism on board, he would have none of it. 'I, who am not a sentimentalist, think it would have been finer if the band of the *Titanic* had been quietly saved, instead of being drowned while playing whatever tune they were playing, the poor devils. I would rather they had been saved to support their families than to see their families supported by the magnificent generosity of the subscribers [to the Heroes Fund] . . . There is nothing more heroic in being drowned very much against your will, off a holed, helpless, big tank in which you bought your passage, than in quietly dying of colic caused by the imperfect salmon in the tin you bought from your grocer.'

But surely this is perverse. No one claimed that everyone who drowned on *Titanic* was a hero: the claim was that *some* were heroic (because others were not) and that some of those were survivors. Moreover, contemporaries thought that one's recorded reaction and conduct during the crisis – whether one helped others at risk to oneself, whether one exhibited composure or panic – was the issue, not the fact of one's death. Those terms seem outmoded nowadays, but only because they have been driven off the public stage into the private realm where conduct in crises and emergencies is still an occasion for shame or sombre pride.

Characteristically, George Bernard Shaw was even more dismissive of any heroism on board *Titanic*. In the London *Daily News* of May 1912, he galloped bumptiously into print. 'What is the first demand of romance in a shipwreck? It is the cry of Women and Children First'. A Titanic lie, claimed Shaw: one boat left with more men than women in it. 'Second romantic demand . . . the captain must be a super-hero, a magnificent seaman, cool, brave . . .'. A Titanic lie: Captain Smith showed bad seamanship in going full-steam into an icefield. 'Third romantic demand. The officers must be calm, proud, steady, unmoved in the intervals of shooting the terrified foreigners'. A Titanic lie: one officer was insubordinate to Ismay. 'Fourth romantic demand. Everybody must face death without a tremor.' A Titanic lie: officers reassured passengers (to avoid panic) when they should have warned them. 'What', asked Shaw, 'is the use of all this ghastly, blasphemous, inhuman, braggartly lying?'

The third romantic demand did incidentally provoke the first version of the Race Question on *Titanic* (I will broach two other versions later) and there were some nastily racist judgements on dark-skinned, non-Anglo-Saxon third-class passengers by survivors. Biel recovers the extent to which *Titanic* and the conduct of its first-class passengers was regarded as exemplary of Anglo-Saxon racial superiority, an attitude which characterised both Americanism and British imperialism. It was being refined and reshaped into British anti-Germanism even at the time, as *Howards End* reminds us.

But this deplorable racism aside, Shaw's logic was mischievously faulty, as Arthur Conan Doyle attempted to show in his replies to Shaw. Doyle pointed out that the officer who was insubordinate was so in the interests of efficiency and safety, thereby proving the opposite of what Shaw wanted to prove. My own objections to Shaw's outburst would, curtly, be these. Shaw rested his first 'lie' on the case of a single lifeboat. The second lie remained debatable at the time. The third was a calumny against most of the officers. The fourth was problematical: Shaw seemed to suggest that realistic panic (and emptiness?) was preferable to orderliness through insincere reassurance: it is a tough judgement call, I would think. Deeper than these was the insult Shaw seemed to deliver to certain memories – that of the band, that of Captain Smith, that of dead officers and engineers. Even had there been a basis for the exposure of alleged (but hardly proven) collective deception (or self-deception), a month after the tragedy was not the time and the Shavian blunderbuss not the weapon.

*

If Forster's concern with the submerged anticipates *Titanic*, Virginia Woolf's concern with submergence (not in a social but an existential sense) seems to have been reinforced if not inspired by the fate of the ship's passengers. *The Voyage Out* (1915), Woolf's first novel, introduces the recurring Woolfian image of the subaqueous (she was in the end to drown herself) and a recent biographer, James King, tells us that 'On 3 May [1912], she and Leonard [her husband] attended the inquiry into the sinking of the *Titanic* on April 14th–15th. The fate of that liner fascinated Virginia.' Indeed it must have, for *The Voyage Out*, which begins with a ship's transatlantic passage to South America, seems to be partially inspired by *Titanic* and her sinking. *Titanic*, after all, was the ship that embarked on 'the voyage out' but did not return, and those who survived her were sea-changed.

Woolf's ship *Euphrosyne* departs with ranked social relationships on board (the stateroom partitions between the travellers are telling) but the novel ends with a lethal individualism not quite balanced by a helpful mutuality. This notion of an atomised society occupied writers of the period and it seems as if Woolf saw *Titanic* as a vivid example of it. E. M. Forster, T. S. Eliot, and Woolf (at the start of her career) thought the best one could do in face of the traditional culture breaking up through cosmopolitanism and individualism was to move between the fracturing parts of society, making connections where possible. The epigraph to *Howards End* was 'only connect' and alluded to purely human connections. Survivors remembered Thomas Andrews, who went down with the ship (that miniature cosmopolis), moving through the stricken liner during its last hours, making human connections where possible. The writers on the whole rejected the modernist notion that society's parts could be welded together through technology that offered speed, size and mechanization as the connections. Andrews' superior, Lord Pirrie, who headed up Harland & Wolff and who missed the maiden voyage through illness, thought this could be applied science's mission. Bulkheads on ships and in society divided people but kept the whole system, ship or society, afloat.

The atomised society is represented on board Woolf's ship, though Woolf has her characters early in the novel dreaming at night of each other, the dreams dissolving the thin partitions that separate them and connecting them strangely at sea. 'What solitary icebergs we are', says one character, 'How little we can communicate.' When field-glasses are trained on *Euphrosyne* from the decks of great liners passing, Woolf's ship becomes a 'an emblem of the loneliness of human life', a 'lonely little island'. Intimations of drowning float ominously in the text, as though death by water were the only possible reunification for the isolated self. Rachel Vinrace gazes with fascination into the depths of the ocean. Her delirium towards the end of the novel produces a vision of her own drowning that I suspect was inspired by Woolf's thoughts about the drowned of *Titanic*: 'She saw nothing and heard nothing but a faint booming sound, which was the sound of the sea rolling over her head. While all her tormentors thought that she was dead, she was not dead, but curled up at the bottom of the sea. There she lay, sometimes seeing darkness, sometimes light, while every now and then someone turned her over at the bottom of the sea.'

In a curious early passage, Woolf depicts England as a shrinking island from the viewpoint of passengers on

departing ships; the description reads like Woolf's trans-
position of survivors' accounts of *Titanic* before she went
under: 'it was a shrinking island in which people were im-
prisoned. One figured them first swarming about like aimless ants, and almost pressing each other over the edge; and
then, as the ship withdrew, one figured them making a vain
clamour, which, being unheard, either ceased, or rose into
a brawl. Finally, when the ship was out of sight of land, it
became plain that the people of England were completely
mute.'

Heroism when it took the popular guise of chivalry was
regarded as a male preserve, but chivalry was being debated
at the time of *Titanic* as part of what we might call the Man
Question, so dubbed by the novelist May Sinclair, writing
in the same 1912 volume of *The English Review* as Conrad. She saw the Man Question as a consequence of the
Woman Question, which the issue of female enfranchise-
ment and the concept of the New Woman together posed.
Sinclair was defending Man against the earlier attack made
on him by Cicely Hamilton in her article 'Man' in the pages
of the same journal. Her defence is considerably more sophisticated than the half facetious reply of someone writing under the pseudonym of 'Homunculus' and who in his
article, 'Woman: A Reply to Man', defends men as lovers
of women and claims that 'Those men were lovers who put
the women in the boats and went down with the Titanic.
They did the noble, the beautiful thing. But a woman is
always the beautiful thing: as girl, as beloved, as mother.
It is her privilege, as the weaker vessel.' The last word is an
odd pun in the circumstances of his example. The oddity is
greater when later in his reply, he likens woman to a ship:
'a woman to us is what a ship is to a sailor – at least, so I

have heard seafaring men say, and they are not bad judges either'. Nowadays, there has been an effort to de-sexualize ships, but the habit is ingrained. Commentators who commit this 'error' are rounded upon by the Politically Correct. A female Professor of Communications in the United States recently referred to a journalist's writing of *Titanic*'s sinking with 'a gash in *her* starboard side' as 'one of the worst sexist violations in print'. The ship's capacity to disturb seems endless!

The self-denying conduct of some men during the sinking gave ammunition to those who thought that chivalry made votes for women unnecessary, and *Howards End* made it clear that not all those were men. We now know that *Titanic* happened in the very middle of the Woman Question in Britain, between the appearance of the New Woman in the mid-1890s (the phrase was coined in 1894) and full adult female suffrage in 1928. Biel discusses the role of *Titanic* in the Woman Question in the United States, and a fuller discussion could likewise be conducted for the British context. Meanwhile, contemporary feminists have looked askance at the scenes on board the sinking *Titanic*. After all, the kind of chivalry alleged to have been demonstrated by male passengers is now spat upon in some quarters (because, it is held, it was a component of a larger, unchivalrous, misogynist social system).

Acts of chivalry (not called that, of course) are committed every day but are quietly and personally acknowledged; this is perhaps a good thing (the trumpeting of chivalry is unpleasant to overhear) though one wonders if a large-scale and protracted (if disorderly) example of chivalry such as the evacuation of female and child passengers from *Titanic* would be possible without the men having a sense of a value system of which chivalry (Women and Children First!) is a part. Without that system, we are dependent on a personal moral inclination arising in the individual man, which may not always be sufficiently strong.

The mechanical unity of society and culture promoted by modernism in such a circumstance as *Titanic* (the kind of unity denied by the writers) used chivalry and the duty of officers and officials as a way of routinely maintaining the unity. Editorializing on the shape a *Titanic* inquiry should take, *The Engineer* of April 19th, 1912, having outlined the technical topics to be covered, printed the following: 'If we have above indicated the direction which some of these inquiries must take, it is through no lack of sympathy with those who are bereaved by the death of kith and kin, nor with the owners of the finest vessel in the world lost on her first voyage; it is because we now feel that it behoves us all to acquit ourselves like men.' Technology and the male standpoint were one and the same, even subliminally so.

Woolf in *The Voyage Out* portrayed the unity breaking down and may well have thought it did so after *Titanic* sank, even if it held until then. It was, of course, the Lifeboat Question that caused the breakdown and showed the limits of chivalry and cooperation in extremity of circumstances. There were insufficient lifeboats on board and those who made it into the boats or on to the backs of the upturned collapsibles were forced to repel with oars or feet the swimmers who tried to clamber to safety and who endangered the others. During and immediately after the sinking the night air was filled with the diminishing cries of those in the ocean. Here were Forster's 'panic and emptiness' with a vengeance. When the understandable behaviour of those who felt imperilled by desperate swimmers came to light later, the disaster took on ominous contemporary tones: chivalry had given way to a Darwinian struggle for survival. I thought immediately of *Titanic* when I read words Conor Cruise O'Brien wrote in 1970 on the theme of the global haves and have-nots (and which he himself quoted in his recent Massey Lectures in Toronto):

> The advanced world may well be like, and feel like, a closed and guarded palace, in a city gripped by the plague. There is another metaphor, developed by Andre Gide, one of the many powerful minds powerfully influenced by Nietzsche: This is the metaphor of the lifeboat, in a sea full of the survivors of a shipwreck. The hands of survivors cling to the sides of the boat. But the boat has already as many passengers as it can carry. No more survivors can be accommodated, and if they gather and cling on, the boat will sink and all will be drowned. The captain orders out the hatchets. The hands of the survivors are severed. The lifeboat and its passengers are saved.

Hans Magnus Enzensberger has invoked a similar metaphor ('the boat is full') when discussing the territorial defence instinct of modern nation states threatened, or perceiving themselves threatened – by immigrant foreigners. There is reason to believe that the *Titanic* experience suggested such grim metaphors or at least fitted them out for use in our century.

H. G. Wells, however, had made use of an earlier occasion when there were insufficient lifeboats: the case of the French frigate *Medusa* en route to Senegal in 1816 when the shipwreck became 'la théâtre de scenes epouvantables'. (Horrible to the point of cannibalism.) Wells drew on this for the opening scenes of *The Island of Dr Moreau* (1896), a horrifying story of restraint abandoned under circumstances of extremity.

This was Joseph Conrad's theme also in *Heart of Darkness* (1902) and I believe it reasserted itself in 1912. For most of his article, 'Some Reflexions, Seamanlike and Otherwise, on the Loss of the Titanic', Conrad sounds like his famous narrator Charlie Marlow resisting manfully the seductive mystique of Mister Kurtz in *Heart of Darkness*. When he assails the British Board of Trade for inadequate supervision of shipbuilding standards, Conrad slides into the tones of Marlow's contempt for the anonymous colonial administrators in Brussels who direct the callous plunder of the Congo Free State: 'A Board of Trade – what is it? A Board of . . . I believe the Speaker of the Irish Parliament is one of the members of it. A ghost. Less than that; as yet a mere memory. An office with adequate and no doubt comfortable furniture.' He deplores what he perceived as the lack of discipline in the building and management of the ship brought about by arrogance and overreach. The last hours of the ship showed him 'the sort of discipline on board these ships, the sort of hold kept on the passengers in the face of the unforgiving sea'; but then discipline was impossible on these 'floating hotels'; command was out of the question. The centre could not hold; things fell apart; anarchy was loosed in crisis: this, put in the terms of W. B. Yeats's great and alarming poem of 1921, 'The Second Coming', was the gist of Conrad's essay.

But this outcome was surely another version of the lack of that restraint that in *Heart of Darkness* Kurtz abandons with what results all readers of the famous novella know. If so, that fateful voyage across the Atlantic by a vessel whose cargo – as Conrad believed – was arrogance and wealth, took place in the fictional universe of Joseph Conrad, novelist, despite the refusal of Joseph Conrad, maritime commentator, to include it among the truly horrifying events of his lifetime.

In the Abyss

It is impossible to be familiar with the literature of the time and not feel reverberations when pondering *Titanic*, both the ship and the calamity. For example, when we think of the highly charged world of the engine-room and boiler-rooms, with their infernal machinery (heat, steam, racket – life below the water-line), it is hard not to think of H. G. Wells' use of such imagery in *The Time Machine*, 'The Cone', 'Lord of the Dynamos' and other stories written a few years before *Titanic* was built, and of which the operating technology of the ship is a curious and real-life enactment.

And there is another Wellsian connection. One of Wells' short stories is 'In the Abyss', the story of the disappearance of a bathyscape in deep water; the explorer fails to return, like the Time Traveller in *The Time Machine* (1895). *Titanic*, found by submersible in a replay of Wells' short story, lies on or near the Sohm Abyssal Plain; and the Abyss is an image of the place *Titanic* sank into: Stygian darkness out of all countenance. Before Ballard proved otherwise, the ship was thought to have suffered extinction of the deepest-dyed kind: 'beyond reach', as the Texan Jack Grimm called the wreck after his failure to find her. It had been assumed by many that volcanic activity in the 1920s had shifted the ocean bed and swallowed the ship – loss upon loss. The poster for *Search for the Titanic* (1980) proclaimed: 'Like a sleeping giant, she has rested for seven decades in the unknown abyss of the North Atlantic'. One imagines with horror the interminable plunge of the *Titanic* with its captives through the darkening ocean; it is the peculiar horror of the *submerged* abyss, of the vast mountains and deep rough valleys that lie *under the ocean, out of sight*.

The fate of *Titanic* brought to culmination the imagery of the Abyss in the late Victorian and Edwardian periods. We find it with its various social, moral, economic, spiritual or psychological meanings, in George Gissing's novel, *The Nether World* (1889), numerous fictions in the 1890s by H. G. Wells, Charles Masterman's *From the Abyss* (1902), Jack London's *People of the Abyss* (1903), Forster's *Howards End* (1910) and Woolf's *The Voyage Out* (1915), among other books. The Abyss is an ancient and powerful notion, but it may have been re-stimulated in Anglo-American imagination by the voyage of the research vessel HMS *Challenger* which traversed over 68,000 miles of sea between 1872 and 1876, plumbing record depths, charting life's bottom-most limit, probing the oceanic abysses.

Wells is especially relevant. In the story of the third-class passengers storming rebelliously upstairs during the sinking of *Titanic*, or of life in the boiler and engine rooms, it is hard not to think (a little guiltily) of the Morlocks in *The Time Machine*, who come up from their underground life to alarm their privileged brothers the Eloi. And the Eloi might remind us (under the circumstances) of those whom Conrad referred to as 'the ineffable hotel exquisites who form the bulk of the first-class Cross-Atlantic passengers'; the ship was considered by some to exhibit a degenerate luxury in first class. And we know that Wells was projecting into the dim future the contemporary and growing gulf between capital and labour.

One *Titanic* legend suggested an even sharper reminiscence of the Morlocks. It was said that as the ship was leaving Queenstown (Cobh), Ireland, the head of a grinning stoker was seen showing above the rim of a funnel (the joker in the stack, one might say): Pratt makes use of this apparition in his poem, 'The Titanic'. The giant funnels might make one think of the shafts to the underground in *The Time Machine*. The stoker reappeared while the ship was sinking, tried to steal the first Marconi operator Jack Phillips' lifebelt, but was floored by Harold Bride, the second Marconi operator, who told the story later. (Pratt used the re-apparition as well.) As Biel explains it, the stoker became 'a grimy stoker of gigantic proportions' in the newspapers' embellishment, and then in Logan Marshall's 1912 book became by racist logic 'a negro stoker' with a knife who clearly intended to kill Phillips for the belt: a dark revenant from below, a Morlock on an obscure embassy of revenge. The expanding story clearly betrayed anxiety of the kind Wells turns to good suspenseful account in his novella, a troubling confusion of the Class and Race questions.

In *Anticipations* (1901), Wells analysed Edwardian society – the here and now – and predicted social reformations in the future, using the language of his fiction, including the image of the Abyss. He borrowed a popular metaphor (perhaps originating with General William Booth) when he referred to the new Urban Poor (the old working class) as 'the "submerged" portion of the social body, a leaderless, aimless multitude of people drifting down towards the abyss'. Immediately above these hapless, he saw the diffuse remnant of the old middle class, 'a vast intricate confusion of different sorts of people, some sailing about upon floating masses of irresponsible property, some buoyed by smaller fragments, some clinging desperately enough to insignificant atoms, a great and varied multitude swimming successfully without aid or with an amount of aid that is negligible in relation to their own efforts, and an equally varied multitude of less capable ones clinging to the swimmers, clinging to the float-ing rich, or clutching empty-handed and thrust and sinking down'. Above these Wells saw the new usurpers of the old aristocracy: 'The most striking of the new classes to emerge is certainly the shareholding class . . . the vast irregular de-velopment of irresponsible wealthy people.'

These three new classes that Wells identified can be rec-ognized in peculiar shorthand on *Titanic*. They seem more accurate than the familiar trio of aristocracy, middle class, and working class. And the social 'deliquescence' that Wells saw at work in Edwardian England (with the Abyss its likely destination for many) received its most graphic unsolicited image in the early hours of April 15th, 1912 when hundreds went to their watery graves.

If we prefer to see the imagery of the Abyss culminating not in the headlong plunge of *Titanic* into the deeps, but in the hellish trenches of the Great War, there is still a connection. The naval rivalry between Germany and Great Britain from 1908 is a backdrop to the building of *Titanic*. Forster uses this rivalry as a component of the impending disaster that haunts *Howards End*. The sinking was a prelude to many sinkings a couple of years later. When war broke out, the ship's sister, *Olympic,* became a troop carrier (as would have *Titanic* pre-sumably had she not met the iceberg), was attacked by a U-boat in 1918, and turned and rammed her tormentor. Another Harland & Wolff White Star liner, *Britannic II*, launched in 1914, was transformed into a hospital ship and was sunk by a mine in the Aegean in November 1916.

Not only the Abyss, but also the surface collision that sent *Titanic* plummeting into it, was a powerful cultural notion with which English writers had already engaged. Thomas Hardy, George Moore and E. M. Forster all depicted unhappy coincidences and the fatal collision of incompatibles in human life. Hardy's cart in *Tess of the d'Urbervilles* (1891) is updated to the motor car in *Howards End*. In *Esther Waters*, metaphoric collisions almost sink the heroine and connect with Moore's depiction of the world of horse-racing and betting as part of the novel's concern with luck (good and bad) in human lives, with how easily fortune (as both wealth and good luck) can become misfortune by the accidental colliding of differences. Passengers collide in Woolf's *The Voyage Out*, as little capable of truly connecting as Forster's characters.

The fate of *Titanic* was a terminal object lesson in – almost indeed a caricature of – what concerned Moore and other writers of the time. The novels of these writers are but tips of the iceberg: late Victorian culture was preoccupied with a universe of chance from which a jealous God seemed to be withdrawing; with a society in which the classes collided more frequently; with a world of mal-adaptation that was, as it were, the everyday reality of evolution; and with an epoch coming to an end not with a whimper but a bang.

A Futurist Event

Titanic, in short, sailed and sank at the very centre of contemporary cultural preoccupations. The ship's size itself ensured this. The ship seemed not just contemporary but futuristic. And writers of the time were engrossed by the benign but also malignant possibilities of the future.

The scale of operation: *Britannic*'s turbine casing

'Titanism' was a literary motif – the future was often imagined as alarmingly grander than the present. We find the
motif of Titanism in Hardy's 1878 novel, *The Return of the
Native* (the 'Titanic forms' of twilit Egdon heath), in Wells'
futuristic novel *When the Sleeper Wakes* (1899), as well as
in Morgan Robertson's anticipation of the building of the
Titanic, his novel *Futility* (1898). Michael McCaughan in
his essay 'Titanicus de Profundis' (in *The Small Titanic,*
a 1994 book about Chris Orr's artwork) quotes Winston
Churchill in 1909: 'We have arrived at a new time – and
with this new time, strange methods, huge forces and com-
binations – a Titanic world – have spread all around us.'

Churchill's world sounds alarming, and indeed danger,
calamity and hazard seemed to be unavoidable portions
of the modernist project of which the ship was a product.
Randall Stevenson reminds us that as early as 1880 the

German philosopher Friedrich Nietzsche was suggesting in 'Premises of the Machine Age' that 'The press, the machine, the railway, the telegraph are premises whose thousand-year conclusion, no one has yet dared to draw.' *Titanic* was not just an immense machine; it was the earth's largest moving manufactured object and it moved with grace and alarming speed. In 1909, the Italian writer F. T. Marinetti published the first *Manifesto of Futurism,* which included the following articles of faith: 'We intend to sing the love of danger, the habit of energy and fearlessness . . . We affirm that the world's magnificence has been enriched by a new beauty: the beauty of speed. A racing car whose hood is adorned with great pipes, like serpents of explosive breath – a roaring car that seems to ride on grapeshot is more beautiful than the *Victory of Samothrace.*'

In 1913 Marinetti listed among contemporary significant phenomena 'Acceleration of life to today's swift pace. Physical, intellectual, and sentimental equilibration on the cord of speed stretched between contrary magnetisms . . . Man multiplied by the machine. New mechanical sense, a fusion of instinct with the efficiency of motors and conquered forces . . . New tourist sensibility bred by ocean liners and great hotels (annual synthesis of different races) . . . Negation of distances and nostalgic solitudes . . . The earth shrunk by speed.' Futurism, he wrote,

is grounded in the complete renewal of human sensibility brought about by the great discoveries of science. Those people who today make use of the telegraph, the telephone, the phonograph, the train, the bicycle, the motorcycle, the automobile, the ocean liner, the dirigible, the aeroplane, the cinema, the great newspaper (synthesis of a day in the world's life) do not realize that the various means of communication, transportation and information have a decisive influence on their psyche.

This was courting danger and the modernist project could clearly unravel or disintegrate. What Herbert Read in 1933 (quoted by Stevenson) said about the art revolution of the day described also the cultural revolution: 'I do think we can already discern a difference of kind in the contemporary revolution: it is not so much a revolution, which implies a turning-over, even a turning-back, but rather a break-up, a devolution, some would say a dissolution. Its character is catastrophic.' The building and launch of *Titanic* followed by its break-up, with all the cultural implications and ramifications, seem almost to have embodied, first the raised hopes and then the dashed hopes of modernism; the catastrophe was in the richest of ways a modernist event.

Stephen Kern reminds us that at the time there were those who voiced passivity and fatalism in the face of this fast-paced predatory future. In 1912 the German novelist Thomas Mann visited his wife in a sanatorium in the Swiss Alps and as a result began that year to write *The Magic Mountain* (1924), a novel about Hans Castorp who visits his cousin in such a sanatorium and ends up staying seven years. It is a study in passive waiting between 1907 and 1914, in rejection of this age of active technology and capitalism. Kern believes the loss of *Titanic* seemed to some to justify pessimism and inaction. Castorp was studying engineering before he arrived at the sanatorium and spent his time reading a book called *Ocean Steamships*.

One of the patients, Settembrini, compared the lives of the patients with the voyage of an ocean liner, and, considering Mann's symbolic intention, the comment also applied to Europe before the war.

The comfort, the luxury, the hubris of tempting fate and controlling the wild elements was a triumph of the human spirit, a 'victory of civilization over chaos', but envious gods may take swift revenge and wreck the luxury liner . . . Settembrini concluded his argument with a suggestive image of Hans, like a small boat, 'flapping about in the gale, head over heels'.

Titanic, Kern adds, 'went down in a calm sea but her stern did flip straight up in the air before the final plunge.'

The *Titanic* Icon

A more positive image of *Titanic* before its loss was generated by the Anglo-American White Star Line Company of Liverpool, ultimately owned by J. P. Morgan and managed by J. Bruce Ismay. In 1987 the Ulster Folk & Transport Museum issued a facsimile of the lively promotional booklet put out by White Star in May 1911: *White Star Line: Royal Mail Triple-Screw Steamers: 'Olympic' and 'Titanic'.* It has been pointed out in *A Question of Murder* that amidst the copious technical and accommodation information in the booklet, safety rated a solitary and isolated line, sadly ironic under the later circumstances, though meant presumably to reassure prospective passengers by its very terseness, as though safety precautions were hardly worth mentioning so unlikely was the opportunity of requiring them. 'The lifeboats, which are 30 feet long, are mounted on special davits on the boat-deck.' Another irony is embedded in this curt line: the special davits referred to were built by a Swedish firm to accommodate tiers of life-boats, not the single boat that in the event hung from each pair of davits.

The vigorous promotion and marketing before the maiden voyage were carried on not just by the White Star Line but also by the engineering and marine engineering journals for which *Titanic* and other great liners were great copy. Pre-voyage promotion and marketing found their counterpart in the international memorabilia industry after the sinking: postcards, posters, booklets, coffee-table books, exhibits. Promotion, the active attempt to sell or 'move' a commodity (remove it profitably from one's possession), became retrospection, the memorializing of an event by keeping in one's possession a relic or replica of it, but a relic or replica collectively desired and itself potentially profitable.

Bown and Simmons tell us that in the Edwardian era 'a national craze of collecting postcards existed in [Britain]'. The craze died away with the outbreak of the Great War – postcard sales dropped dramatically with the rise in postage rates and increased use of the telephone. The collecting craze returned in the 1970s and 'amongst the most sought after postcards are those depicting the "Titanic". The rarest cards are those that were issued and posted before the date of the disaster. After April 15th, 1912, postcard publishers issued a wide variety of postcards.' There were also memorial postcards issued immediately after the sinking and which functioned as relics of the tragedy. Many of these cards were pseudo-religious. Michael McCaughan drew my attention to 1912 *Titanic* memorial postcards inspired by religious art although by the stylized postures of the depicted maidens they appear to have been influenced by the Edwardian stage and early motion pictures.

The sincere outpourings of grief were increasingly manufactured, yet the sentimental religiosity in which the event swam welled up from deep and disturbing notions, including that of the waiting Abyss, which was not just the secular literary image of crisis in English society that I have

Titanic memorial postcard

mentioned but one that derived from the Bible and ancient
pictures of hell and purgatory. The ship lay, as it were, in
the Christian Abyss (with the 'souls' all ship's carried), in
Milton's 'darkness visible'. The *Titanic* sinking dramatically
reactivated the Christian Lifeboat metaphor which was very
different from André Gide's referred to by Cruise O'Brien.
We meet this metaphor in General William Booth's 1890
exposé of London poverty, *In Darkest England*. In his book
he devotes a chapter to those 'On the Verge of the Abyss'
and refers to the 'sinking classes' whom the Salvation Army
is especially interested in saving. It seems to me likely that
Forster derived these very metaphors in *Howards End* from
Booth's book (or from Booth via Wells); and there is a running nautical metaphor in Forster's novel, that of 'the ropes
of life' on which some have their hands and others, alas, do
not and sink as a consequence.

Booth's answer to these social problems is the 'Salvation Ship', of which *Titanic* could be seen as a sad travesty,

especially in the light of the numbers of poor European and Irish emigrants it carried. The answer is certainly not, he argued, *laissez faire*, the laws of human supply and demand. How do these principles look 'when we apply them to the actual loss of life at sea? Does "Let things alone" man the lifeboat? . . . No desire to make it pay created the National Lifeboat Institution . . . We want a Social Lifeboat Institution, a Social Lifeboat Brigade, to snatch from the abyss those who, if left to themselves, will perish as miserably as the crew of a ship that founders in mid-ocean.'

The technical and social *hubris* that contemporary commentators identified in the case of *Titanic* accorded with the Christian idea of retribution: this was God in the guise of Nature putting Man in his place. That more poor people (many of them presumably good Christians, certainly many of the Irish poor would have been pious Catholics) were put in their place than rich would not have fazed the fundamentally religious. 'God Himself could not sink this ship', a woman passenger recalled a crewman telling her, though we have to take the utterance of the remark on trust. An engineering journal of the time said rather that the ship's construction made it 'practically unsinkable', a rather different assessment and devoid of anything more than a little complacency. But for many it was clearly an occasion for God's payback. Michael McCaughan in 'Titanicus de Profundis' quotes the Bishop of Winchester who saw in the disaster 'a monument and warning to human presumption'. (Conrad had much the same interpretation but from a strictly secular point of view.)

On a lesser scale, the disaster was thought to teach the lesson that warnings should be heeded. Captain Smith, having been told of icebergs in his path, was judged not to have heeded the information, paying the penalty and causing hundreds of others to pay along with him. Stephen Kern has seen it as a case of wilful blindness and a study in the contemporary reordering of the world in terms of time and space. A new intense value placed on time and speed led to recklessness. In Kern's reading, Smith's behaviour was cultural rather than personal. 'The age', he writes, 'had its doubts and hesitations, but it was essentially characterized by hubris that ignored the warning messages and pushed the throttle full speed ahead.' He even sees the loss of *Titanic* as 'a simile for the outbreak of the war' two years later. The short-sightedness of the lookouts, the lack of safety precautions, the reliance on technology, the overweening confidence, the flurry of wireless messages, even the icebergs in the path of the liner – Kern finds larger scale analogies in the July crisis of 1914 that precipitated the catastrophe of the Great War.

Sometimes it is not thought to be anything as grand as *hubris* that caused warnings to be ignored but mere incompetence. (This was the view of the American politicians at the time.) The truth of the allegation aside, this 'lesson' of *Titanic* has in the intervening decades taken on an independent existence and the ship is in some circumstances an icon of folly. For amusement I draw attention to a 1994 example. In that year an 18-minute documentary, *The Titanic*, was produced in the United States by Standard Chartered at a trial in which that company sought damages from the accounting firm of Price Waterhouse. The video compares the accounting firm to *Titanic* and alternates information and graphics with footage from *A Night to Remember*. In the final scene of the video, the liner slips beneath the waves while the narrator intones: 'Price Waterhouse had numerous warnings United Bank was in troubled waters but also chose not to listen.

Perhaps they too thought they were invincible.' It seems that the video has already established cult status in American business circles. That it has done so suggests that a certain playfulness in the analogy has been recognized, a postmodernist game with images. On the other hand, *Howards End* depicted financial crisis as an intimation of more general cultural collapse, and the gamesmanship of capitalism is shown as having serious, even fatal consequences.

Interestingly, the aura of piety (in another before-and-after parallel) was revived after 1985, since some people, including Robert Ballard, have seen removal of items from the wreck not just as vandalism but as desecration. In two expeditions, in 1987 and 1993, about 2,600 objects were recovered from the debris field. Two hundred items from that trove were put on display in 1994–95 at the National Maritime Museum in Greenwich: all were in a good state of preservation due to the dark, cold conditions in which they had reposed. This exhibition was roundly attacked by many who regard the ship as a religious monument or icon and the salvage of objects as 'grave-robbing', the more so since the U.S. Congress had declared the area of the ship a Memorial Site. Stephen Low offers his version of this in *Titanica*, which encourages us to see the wreck as a mausoleum, and its debris field as a submarine cemetery, holy Judea-Christian ground.

Inside this aura, of course, are contested hard-nosed legalities, rivalries, and ethics of salvage. The most celebrated rivalry is between RMS Titanic, a New York salvage company that has been legally awarded exclusive rights to the sunken ship, and Robert Ballard, discoverer of the wreck and who believes that the site should be preserved from commercial interference. (Those exclusive rights were awarded on condition that the integrity of the wreck is maintained, though this didn't prevent the recent failed attempt amidst huge publicity to bring to the surface a piece of the hull.) But the amiable Ballard has been called 'a high-tech cowboy' who pits a maverick enterprise against the corporate enterprise of RMS Titanic: two ways of being profitably in the limelight, two ways of being American with a hard nose. Like many Americans, Ballard has a 'vision' or 'dream', in his case a desire to create an underwater museum. His recent discovery of the wreck of *Britannic*, related in a Nova television documentary, *Titanic's Lost Sister* (1997), has given him his latest opportunity since he was foiled in the cases of *Titanic* (legally beyond him now) and *Lusitania* (too broken up). But surely the commercial sharks will now be attracted to the Aegean by the scent of money and it is hard to believe that even if there is a *Britannic* underwater museum, it will not – especially if certain Americans have anything to do with it – be there primarily to make tourist dollars.

To the extent that genuine piety attaching to *Titanic* has been drowned by vested interests, one might almost imagine the ship as a symbol of sunken popular Protestantism after it had shored up the Victorian, imperial states of the West, particularly England and the United States. It is as if Protestantism was overwhelmed by the very capitalism it had once encouraged. At the time, the aura of piety was enhanced by the story (that became a kind of folk belief) that as the ship went down the band played 'Nearer My God to Thee'. Others have it that it was in fact the even more appropriate Protestant hymn, 'Autumn', which contains the lines

> Hold me up in mighty waters,
> Keep my eyes on things above.

Lord thinks it might actually have been a popular waltz, 'Songe d'Automne', simply called 'Autumn' by English speakers. But the events of April 14th–15th, 1912 quickly became legendary in any case. According to Stephen Low, it was rumoured at the time that a worker was lost during the building of the ship and his body entombed in the ship's structure. (I have heard the figure of 17 as the number of men killed while working on the ship are mentioned, but surely this is urban folklore.) When I heard this I couldn't help recalling the R. J. Welch photograph in which a workman has been crudely erased, leaving a ghostly, plasmic presence; perhaps Welch removed the figure himself, wishing to show more of the starboard tail shaft, but it gives one a queer feeling nonetheless.

Fitting tail-shaft to *Titanic*: a ghostly presence

The Lore and Lure of *Titanic*

The history of *Titanic* is an episode in the history of the outlandish. According to Ralph White, cameraman on the 1985 French-American search team, the wreck would not have been discovered had members of the team not been previously involved in the Search for the Loch Ness Monster project.

The legendry enveloping the ship has not abated. After the event, dozens of premonitions of the disaster were claimed. The most famous was perhaps the celebrated survivor Eva Hart's repeated statement that her mother had such a premonition of disaster that she refused to sleep during the voyage. So many reports of premonitions were there that George Behe collected and classified them in *Titanic: Psychic Forewarnings of a Tragedy* (1988). And after the disaster there have been what we might by analogy call 'postmonitions', sightings or sensings that warn, as it were, after the fact or carry the spirit of the original premonitions through the foretold event itself into its afterlife.

Even if the stories behind the recent American tabloid's claim that 'the specter of a huge ocean liner has been sighted at least a dozen times during the past three years and hundreds of times since it sank' is full of elementary errors, the *fact* of the story is evidence of the saleable legendry of the ship. The captain of the Norwegian trawler whose crew four summers ago saw the ship – on the surface of the ocean *but in its present sunken* condition – is named and quoted, with that semi-corroboration we find in folklore of this kind, and in which ghost ships recur as actors. In this particular sighting, *Titanic* appears as the folkloric Ship of Death, or the spectral sailing ship of Samuel Taylor

Coleridge's 'The Ancient Mariner' translated into the age of steam. After the sinking, it was easy to believe, too, that the ship had sailed under some kind of curse; it was said that the priestess of Thebes had cast a curse on anyone who disturbed her remains and yet the British were recklessly sending her to the U.S.

Intriguing in a way that might have caught the attention of Oscar Wilde with his claim that life imitates art (there was a Chief Officer Wilde on board, who went down with the ship and was said to be the bravest of men), is the fact that there were a curious number of imaginative anticipations of the ship and its fate. In *A Night to Remember,* Lord exhumed Morgan Robertson's 1898 novel, *Futility*, about a fabulous Atlantic liner that while filled with rich and complacent people hits an iceberg one April night and sinks. The specifications of the real *Titanic* were almost identical to those of Robertson's fictional liner which was, incredibly, called the *Titan*.

Wade has salvaged other anticipations, including a short story by Mayn Clew Garnett that was being printed as *Titanic* prepared for her maiden voyage. Then there was the American Celia Thaxter's 1874 poem entitled 'A Tryst', that anticipates both the fate of the liner and Hardy's far superior verse response to it:

> From out the desolation of the North
> An iceberg took it away,
> From its detaining comrades breaking forth,
> And traveling night and day . . .
>
> Like some imperial creature, moving slow,
> Meanwhile, with matchless grace,

> The stately ship, unconscious of her foe,
> Drew near the trysting place.

It is possible that Hardy had read Thaxter, and that he had also read the poem 'The Berg; A Dream' (1988) by Herman Melville, the American author of *Moby-Dick*. In Melville's poem, an 'impetuous' ship is foolishly steered into an ice-berg 'bound for death' and, 'stunned', sinks 'in bafflement'. The 'slimy slug' that sprawls along the 'dead indifference' of the iceberg's walls is very like Hardy's 'sea-worm' that crawls, 'slimed, dumb, indifferent' inside the wreck. But 'the convergence of the twain' was a major motif in Hardy's work from the beginning, which lessens the impact of any borrowing: he, like the others, had before 1912 already im-agined the *Titanic*.

And like Thaxter, Hardy had imagined the ship as alive, almost human, and this is a feature of the *Titanic* legend that surpasses the conventional feminizing of ships. The ship is the protagonist in a drama, but because the iceberg was antagonist, it too has been animated by these two poets. Melville in his dream felt the 'dankish breath' of the berg. E. J. Pratt goes farther and in some striking lines imagines the southward voyaging berg as losing gradually its archi-tectural (i.e. civilized) appearance and reverting to animal form, until

> nothing but the brute
> And palaeolithic outline of a face
> Fronted the transatlantic shipping route.

It lurches and shambles 'like a plantigrade' and the lair it stumbles back to is the point of collision with *Titanic*. Sure-

ly Pratt has re-imagined W. B. Yeats's 'rough beast' slouch-
ing towards some new Bethelehem, 'its hour come round at
last'. If so, then he has added one more twentieth-century
event to those we know kindled Yeats to imagine the birth
of a new and terrible dispensation for humankind.

In a more scientific and yet still imaginative key, the
Canadian Richard Brown has written a peculiar but fascinating book entitled *Voyage of the Iceberg: The Story of
the Iceberg that Sank the Titanic* (1983), which gives the
villain of the piece a life of its own before and after the fatal
collision with the liner. This is a collision between nature
and man, natural history and human history, seen from the
unusual point of view, as it were, of the berg. Nature easily
absorbs the human in Brown's story. The iceberg is the hero
of Brown's book, with *Titanic* 'only a supporting character
in a cast of ships, seals and whales, bears and seabirds, and
men as well', during the berg's 'long voyage down to the
Grand Banks', but in that unusual spring of 1912 melting to
nothing only 300 miles north of Bermuda.

There is a well-known photograph, of course, of the likely
culprit taken on April 15th from a German ship; observ-
ers noted a scar of red paint guiltily striping the side of the
iceberg. Perhaps Brown's book provoked the clever spoof
article by Paul LeBlond and Donald Hodgins in *The Journal of Irreproducible Results*, 'Iceberg Psychodynamics'
(1984), demonstrating by a 'bergocentric' reference frame
that 'icebergs *do* have minds of their own', however mod-
estly evolved. The article might be an irreverent gloss on
the so-called pathetic fallacy of the various poets by which
inanimate objects are given human features.

*

86

The impact of the sinking was as great in the United States as in Britain and Ireland – if anything, greater. Curiously, although black journalists in the United States paid scant attention to the disaster, it became of peculiar significance to black Americans on the street. To them, the ship was a symbol of white racist society: its building was a monument to white *hubris* and its foundering was meet retribution for the mistreatment of black people. In one introduction to his song, 'Titanic', the famous bluesman Leadbelly said there were no black passengers on the ship, that Jack Johnson, the world heavyweight champion, tried to board but was told by Captain Smith, 'I ain't haulin' no coal'. In the song, Johnson is safe on dry land and in bitter glee bids the *Titanic* fare thee well. It was *because* the ship carried no blacks (and perhaps because, paradoxically, no black people were permitted to share the trumpeted fate of the rich whites) that *Titanic* hosted this second version of The Race Question whether she would or no.

Perhaps 'Smith's' derogatory word for blacks, combined with the importance of coal to the ship (she carried 5,000 tons of it: some of it helps to compose the debris field today), stimulated the 'Titanicisation' of a figure already active in black urban folklore. This was Shine (his name presumably from Shoeshine or because he was so black he shone), who was reborn as the mythical black stoker aboard *Titanic,* a case of anecdotal white lore (the journalistic report of the 'negro' stoker who tried to steal Jack Phillips's life-belt) being absorbed – in a kind of collective homeopathic revenge – by a strong existing folk tradition.

Shine as we know from the researches of Roger Abrahams is a kind of Trickster, and hero of a species of long narrative poem called the 'Toast' (not unrelated to rap, jive-talk, the talking blues, and the rhythmic, rhyming street-banter called 'the dozens'). In it, Shine is the only passenger or crewman capable of swimming from the sinking vessel and in belated revenge he refuses to help the white folks, even in return for the promise of all those things white people thought black people coveted (including 'all the pussy eyes ever did see'). In Leadbelly's song, when the white folks go under, Jack Johnson is on shore dancing the Eagle Rock. In one version of the *Titanic* Toast,

> when all them white folks went to heaven,
> Shine was in Sugar Ray's bar drinking Seagram's Seven.

In some other Toasts, Shine makes a descent into Hell, a mythic parallel to his usual situation on earth, labouring in the boiler and engine rooms of the liner. Etheridge Knight, the black American poet, has a loosened-up (but not cleaned-up) version of the Toast in his poem, the mock-Whitmanesque 'I Sing of Shine'.

The ship has figured in white lore, too, both oral and printed. For example, there were innumerable jokes; a later example: Lady Astor: 'I asked for ice in my drink but this is ridiculous.' This joke draws upon the reports that some first-class passengers popped some iceberg splinters into their drinks, but confuses the American-born, British Nancy, Viscountess Astor (who made regular appearances in British jokes, perhaps in male revenge against her strong temperance advocacy, her feminism and her appeasement of Germany before the Second World War) with John Jacob's young bride. For their part, political cartoonists have frequently put the disaster to satirical use, in what amounts to a kind of journalists' lore. The sinking has been a god-send to cartoonists who wish to depict sinking careers and shipwrecked policies. A recent example is a cartoon in the Vancouver *Sun* in January 1994 attacking the Canadian Finance Minister and captioned 'Karaoke Sing-a-long on the S.S. Titanic'. *The Times* of London of December 12th, 1996 carried a cartoon showing a cabinet minister in civvies jumping off the stern of *Titanic* while on deck a glum Prime Minister John Major and another cabinet minister (both in officer uniform) look on.

There is a material equivalent of *Titanic* folklore in those bars and hostelries displaying relics and replicas as decoration. An almost random example would be Tom Bergin's – 'the House of Irish Coffee' – in Los Angeles which regularly features the Titanic Jazz Band: 'Traditional Jazz: Tuesday Evenings'. *Titanic* relics, photographs, framed newspaper stories, etc. compose a useful and readymade decor within a general nautical theme that accords with British-style pubs. One English pub has entire lounge sections that were originally on *Titanic*'s sister ship *Olympic* and one Liverpool hotel has serious *Titanic* memorabilia on display. Perhaps at work is a faint subliminal hint of danger which is not unwanted in a pub where talk, hard drinking, and flirting go on, and all being conducted in the lightly suggested ambience of *Titanic*'s floating urbanity.

Titanic museums are more formal versions of this display of hardware, and there are several dedicated to the ship, including The Titanic Memorial Museum, Inc., Sidney, Ohio; Titanic Museum, Heritage Waterfront Park, Fall River, Massachusetts; The Titanic Museum, Bad Wildungen, Germany. The affix 'Inc.' reminds us of the American interplay between the generous impulse to disseminate information and the impulse to make generous money. Many general purpose museums have recently mounted *Titanic* exhibits, including museums in Los Angeles, Vancouver and Belfast. The salvage – or plunder, some would say – of RMS Titanic Inc. has given *Titanic* exhibits a new and profitable lease of life. The largest exhibition of *Titanic* artifacts will be in Memphis, Tennessee in 1997, the latest in the high-powered *Memphis Wonders* series; the catalogue will be lavish and business of all kinds brisk. *Titanic* and tourism will softly collide and neither sink.

The business of *Titanic* memorabilia has also been brisk. What is contemporary with the disaster (objects of the time) and therefore somehow genuine has been followed, during the waves of *Titanic* enthusiasm, by manufactured copies or spin-offs. For example, when the ship sank, there was a Memorial Handkerchief produced, a keepsake that could also supposedly be used by the bereaved; this handkerchief has recently been re-issued by Scouse Press in Liverpool, which also puts out a *Titanic* Grief Kit containing the 1912 records, including the premiere recording of *The Wreck of the Titanic* (the 1912 Descriptive Piano Solo). It is all, as the Press smilingly admits, 'in the very best of bad taste'. Michael McCaughan's booklet, *Titanic* (Ulster Folk & Transport Museum, 1982), deliberately imitates the original White Star promotional booklet and thereby treads the passage from hard-sell commodification to the cult of nostalgia, from modernity to post-modernity. A Southampton firm, Rembrandt, offers for sale *Titanic* 'Souvenirs, Covers, Postcards, Survivors [*sic*] Signatures, Menu, Badges, Soons [Spoons?], Key Fob, Models etc.'.

Although certain memorabilia may be exact reproductions of contemporary items, and therefore identical, they are in fact subtly and radically different, since they are offered and received in a transparent envelope of self-consciousness, their meaning sea-changed by context and the intervening years. I am reminded of Jorge Luis Borges' remarkable story, 'Pierre Menard, Author of the *Quixote*'. In this story a modern writer writes *Don Quixote*. It is identical, word for word, to Cervantes' 17th-century novel, *Don Quixote*, but is nevertheless held to be subtly different from Cervantes' work and superior to it. We might say that it has the superior knowingness of posterity, even of nostalgia, that in our time *Titanic* allows us to imagine and indulge.

*

The internationalism of the *Titanic* complex, then, is quite extraordinary. It is further (and perhaps gratuitously) evidenced by the number of flourishing Titanic Historical Societies in various countries. The premier society is in Indian Orchard, Massachusetts (Titanic Historical Society, Inc., 1974, formed from Titanic Enthusiasts of America, 1963), but there are numerous others, including The British Titanic Society, Titanic International and The Titanic Society of South Africa. Titanic societies are normally serious conclaves, similar to local history societies, devoted to a narrow subject but across fields of interest and walks of life. They belong to the history of clubs, enthusiasms and pastimes. (There is an interest in *Titanic* at the level of parlour game, for the ship and its fate are complicated and detailed enough to support a sustained 'trivial pursuit'.) Such societies are also custodians of the ship's legends and are often loose enough to accommodate the buffs and freaks who inhabit the no-man's-land between technological enthusiasm and devotional fanaticism.

Titanic addicts have recently found a new and happy

hunting ground, the green pastures of the Internet. There they sport among *Titanic* websites and home pages. Newcomers will quickly find a Titanic Internet Historical Association which generates 30 to 80 e-mail messages daily; in front of the monitor, mouse in hand, participating in news groups, one can almost imagine oneself a Jack Phillips or Harold Bride of the late twentieth century. Web searchers will find 'Titanic: Adventure Out of Time', a computer version of the old semi-obsolete parlour game: 'the new interactive game from *Cyberflix, Inc.* and GTE *Entertainment* sends you back to 1912 as an espionage agent onboard the doomed luxury liner . . . learn about the facts and legends surrounding the sinking, check out conspiracy theories, and meet the Edwardian glitterati (that's beautiful People to you and me) in our Titanic Star Telegraph.'

No one can dispute the research value and potential of the Internet to the *Titanic* student; even the game above comes barnacled with data about the ship and her fate. Watching *Titanic's Lost Sister* and wondering how Frank Prentice, the surviving crewman, spelled his name, I stepped to my study and in a hundred seconds had brought his name and precise occupation on board ship up on screen. The trick is to shut the computer off when you have your answer and save yourself from drowning in a veritable ocean of information where perspective and interpretation seem unnecessary. The same trick is equally useful when one is foolhardy to write about the global phenomenon we call *Titanic*.

PART II

Bringing It All Back Home

Titanic City

The city that built *Titanic* may have once participated in the noise, glamour, controversy, and potent various meanings of the ship and what befell it, but that participation was short-lived. That explains why only recently has the city of Belfast come to the attention of those intrigued by *Titanic* but who are not among the *Titanic* cognoscenti who know virtually all there is to know, factually at least, about the ship. Even among the real enthusiasts, Belfast is simply where the vessel was created; once she was launched, the city's shipyards for them become as empty and uninteresting as the abandoned nest from which the bird has fledged and flown, never to return. But as the city where the heroic form of *Titanic* was raised, Belfast repays a closer look. Belfast, after all, is where the international cultural phenomenon of *Titanic* began.

This neglect of Belfast, Titanic City, is not just international but local: only now are the citizens of Belfast awakening to the cultural significance for them of that great liner and others their fellow citizens of yesteryear designed, built, fitted out, and then launched into the great world. There were island-wide reasons for this neglect. One had to do with the kind of culture that is regarded as authentically Irish. Up until now, the applied science culture of Belfast has seemed to disqualify itself as of the culture of Ireland. There are also reasons that originated in Britain, having to do with the kind of activity that is regarded as authentically cultural: up until now, industrialism (even when it has produced impressive collective artifacts) has seemed to disqualify itself. Besides, once the heroic days of steamships (and the less heroic days of linen and other manufacture) were over by the mid-twentieth century, Belfast declined into an unremarkable provincialism and became a city wearing only the mask of a city, to borrow the novelist James Joyce's description of early twentieth-century Dublin.

The fraught political situation of the time did not help, either. The monumental achievements of the east Belfast shipyards, particularly of Harland & Wolff, were complicated by the deep political and religious divisions of the city's population, even of the shipyards' workforce. One result of those radical divisions was the partition of Ireland in 1920–1921 into the Irish Free State and Northern Ireland. The constitutional status of the region of Ireland of which Belfast became capital in 1921 (the devolved statelet of Northern Ireland) prevented Belfast from continuing to display the cultural potency of Liverpool and Glasgow, cities that had played a comparable maritime role in the later Industrial Revolution. For ongoing and complicated political reasons, Northern Ireland was complicit in its own low profile. The retrospective celebration of *Titanic* as a triumph of visionary marine engineering was a casualty in the new dispensation after 1921: increasingly, on hindsight, it was associated with one portion of the population (the unionists or Protestants) and dissociated from the other (the nationalists or Catholics). Indeed, it was assumed with justification that *some* nationalists in Ireland were not displeased by what was seen not just as the *Titanic* disaster but the disaster of *Titanic*. The net result of all these factors was a politic silence where the great ship was concerned.

In any case, who with a vested interest in the selling and building of ships wished to dwell on the disaster of April 15th, 1912? It instantly became a notorious ship that elicited ambiguous pride and embarrassment in the city that built her. The decades' long official reticence about the ship began at least as early as March 4th, 1913 when the White Star Line wrote to Father Browne when they learned that he was presenting an illustrated lecture to appreciative audiences. They requested him to desist 'as we do not wish the memory of this calamity to be perpetuated'.

After the civil unrest in Northern Ireland (Ulster) began around a quarter century ago, *Titanic* sank deeper not just in the Northern Irish mind but also in the minds of those abroad fascinated by *Titanic* yet disinclined to show interest in a city by then associated solely and cruelly with a vicious low-intensity civil war. Only recently has Belfast surfaced as a city worth celebrating as the home of *Titanic* and – I am at pains to add in this short book – of other vast products of modernity. Indeed, it seems that the ship's builders, Harland & Wolff, were for some time loath to associate themselves with research into, or commemoration of, *Titanic*, for understandable reasons. But perhaps the decline of shipbuilding in Belfast, the historical nature of the *Titanic* event, its inescapable popularity abroad, and current assumption into commemorative culture, have all dissipated corporate fear that association with tragedy is bad for business. Today *Titanic* is good for anybody's business.[2]

Yet all along, *Titanic* worked its passage in Ulster culture and the Ulster psyche, sometimes in plain sight, at other times clandestinely. I want to relate its readily accessible meanings to the international pattern of response to the ship and its loss that I have already revealed, and to uncover some of its less accessible or less familiar meanings for the Irish.

Shipwrights and Playwrights

Northern Ireland, for example, has produced its share of art inspired by *Titanic*. Two notable paintings, Charles Dixon's 'Titanic Fitting Out at Belfast' (1912) and William Conor's 'Men of Iron' (1922), are on display at the permanent *Titanic* exhibit at the Ulster Folk and Transport Museum, Cultra, County Down. A more recent painting by Ken Robbie depicts the ship's departure from Belfast, April 2nd, 1912. Increasingly, Ulster enthusiasts are focusing on the birth and baptismal dates of the ship, not the date of her death. This seems right and proper, for the achievement of the ship has been unfairly (if understandably) eclipsed by the sensational

---

2 Witness the current American advertisement for Sonicare, a 'sonic frequency' tooth brush. 'If sonic technology can find THE TITANIC two miles below the ocean, why not use it to reach plaque bacteria just BELOW THE GUMLINE?' The pitch surrounds a photograph of the sunken ship, looking like a large grey molar, perhaps even a bacterium-eaten ship (remembering the recent discovery of the steel-consuming bacterium down there).

and historic nature of her loss. (Though one must be careful that local pride does not become the very provincialism that the building of the ship implicitly in its modernity denied.)

Good literature inspired by *Titanic* has been rather more substantial. The well-known east Belfast playwright and Abbey Theatre (Dublin) manager St John Ervine in his play *The Ship* (staged in 1922, but quite Edwardian in its feel) unmoors *Titanic* from Belfast and tows it, as it were, to Biggport, a fictional English port. Set in its future, the play imagines *Titanic* and *Olympic*, both of which are named in the text, being superseded by the oil-driven *Magnificent* under construction by John Thurlow. Thurlow as a character is perhaps inspired by several shipbuilders associated with Belfast – Sir Edward Harland, who made Harland & Wolff a great yard, Lord Pirrie who assumed sole control of the Yard in 1906, and Thomas Andrews; behind them all might stand the Norwegian playwright Henrik Ibsen's *Master Builder*. *Magnificent* strikes an iceberg on her maiden voyage to New York and amidst great loss of life takes Thurlow's son down with her.

Ervine seeks in his play to depict the victimisation of the young by the old, of natural inclination by iron will, of nature by mechanization. Somehow the ship's loss is the fruit of Thurlow's *hubris,* which is also the *hubris* of the machine culture in which machinery is morally idle even when mechanically active. *Magnificent* is a 'floating hotel', the very phrase Conrad and others had used to demean *Titanic*. Modernity is offered at its worst in the Great War (in which machines, unlike great liners, are designed to kill) but Ervine nevertheless couples the machines of war with *Titanic*. The problem with the play is that the audience would have foreseen the dramatic climax, would have seen the iceberg coming, through the very resemblance of events to the *Titanic* story that generated the play in the first place. Despite the *hubris* and catastrophe, Ervine tries unsuccessfully at the last moment to reverse engines in the action's looming future by salvaging the building of great ships as somehow redemptive and shipbuilding dynasties as noble. This may have been Ervine's residual Ulster Scots pride churning into reverse too late in order to avoid the interpretation of the *Titanic* disaster that most writers felt literature obliged them to advance.

The story of *Titanic* is its own iceberg that sinks this workmanlike play. Nevertheless, *The Ship* bravely takes on board some significant cultural and ethical issues that were raised by the real ship and its fate: the ultimate desirability of machinery; the morality of machine-driven pleasure; the culpability of modernity in twentieth-century havoc. But in order to close with these issues, Ervine obviously, wrongly, and provincially thought he had to remove the story out of Belfast to the 'mainland', thereby losing the opportunity of rescuing the drama from a sub-Ibsenite vapidity.

Fifty-two years later, *The Iceberg,* a radio play by the late east Belfast playwright Stewart Parker, was broadcast on the BBC. It uses contemporary reports of men killed during the ship's construction by having as its central figures two dead workers. Parker uses also the 'descent into hell' motif (i.e. descent into the boiler and engine rooms). This is a good effort but perhaps, though, the two workmen are too reminiscent of Samuel Beckett's Vladimir and Estragon in *Waiting for Godot,* and Tom Stoppard's Rosencrantz and Guildenstern in *Rosencrantz and Guildernstern are Dead*, to let this early Parker play truly succeed. The play might have done for one archetypal event in Ulster loyalist psycho-history what Frank McGuinness did for the other in his play, *Observe the Sons of Ulster Marching Towards the Somme* (1986), but is not densely enough textured to do so. The Ulster *Titanic* play has yet to be written.

Ulster poets have not been as drawn to the disaster as we might have expected. Samuel K. Cowan published a heartfelt but artistically indifferent loyalist ode, 'De Profundis', in *From Ulster's Hills* (1913). John Hewitt in his sonnet 'Late Spring, 1912' *(Kites in Spring*, 1980) has some poignant lines on his memory of reading as a five year-old the news of the sinking on the newsboy's bill (I can't but think of the newsboy in Welch's photograph), but it was only one episode in a season of bad news (Scott of the Antarctic likewise foundered amidst ice). In 'Death of an Old Lady' (1956), Louis MacNeice wove into his elegy for his stepmother his 'one shining glimpse' of *Titanic* as she steamed down Belfast Lough to the sea and combined this with the iceberg as a metaphor for the old lady's own sinking. Memories of *Titanic* being launched and leaving Belfast were privately cherished for decades after. The producer of *A Night to Remember*, William MacQuitty of Belfast, was one eyewitness. So was the renowned Belfast-born ornithologist, scholar, and Anglican priest, Edward A. Armstrong, who recalled the experience in his beautiful memoir *Birds of the Grey Wind* (1940): 'I was a little boy when my father took me on board the *Titanic* as she lay in dock. I mischievously cut off a sliver of woodwork from the gangway as a memento, though I could not know then that a few months later she would lie at the bottom of the sea, having carried fifteen hundred men, women, and children, to their doom on her maiden trip.' Armstrong was surely among the first to have a memento of *Titanic* turn into a relic of the ship.

The best local poem I know on the subject is 'Bruce Ismay's Soliloquy', later re-titled by the poet 'After the *Titanic*'. The author is that excellent poet Derek Mahon and those familiar with his work know that he is characteristically attracted to the lost (and in this case reviled) figure amidst the crowd. Ismay takes his place among the deserted places and abandoned or expelled people in Mahon's distinctive landscape. The disgraced manager speaks from his exile in those posthumous tones of which Mahon is so fond. Derek Mahon has found a niche in Titanica which as a Belfastman he can occupy without compromising his maverick rejection of regional pride. In the poem, Ismay strikingly recalls (in a Mahonesque blend of the homely detail, the punning metaphor, and the hollow existence), that

> As I sat shivering on the dark water
> I turned to ice to hear my costly
> Life go thundering down in a pandemonium of
> Prams, pianos, sideboards, winches,
> Boilers bursting and shredded ragtime.

Robert Johnstone addresses the same episode in his impressive suite of poems, '*Titanic*', in *Eden to Edenderry* (1989):

> all the innards slid forward and down:
> the boilers and the turbine came adrift.
> Its organs loose, the ship gutted itself.[3]

---

3 It has been recently claimed that the noise of rumbles and roars that survivors heard from their lifeboats was a 'brittle fracture' in the ship's steel hull rather than the shifting of gear and boiler explosions.

Johnstone uses as epigraph for his suite lines from Enzens-berger's *The Sinking of the Titanic,* neatly connecting for us the local with the international. For Johnstone the wreck and its discovery excite nightmares, misshapen extrusions of a troubled psyche. The personal 'soul voyage' in 'Not an Explosion but a Crash' ('size had magnetised the ship to troubles') becomes in 'Undertakers' the collective, feverish soul-voyage of a riven society like Northern Ireland's.

While nothing comparable to the folklore of Shine devel-oped in Belfast, *Titanic* spread from historical fact into the general and potent folklore of a shipyard which has been a source of serious pride, deflationary humour, and even urban identity for the inhabitants of industrial (and now largely post-industrialist) east Belfast. Belfast citizens are not above a joke at their own expense: 'Did you know Belfast built the world's largest submarine?' 'No jokin'?' 'Aye, it was called the *Titanic!*' Beyond Belfast, the folklore of the ship took the form of the traditional ballad (McCaughan quotes one from County Fermanagh), nine of which were known to D.K. Wilgus, who found that the Irish songs tend to praise the ship and its crew while the American songs belabour them.

Another local version of response abroad has been the launch in 1992 of the Ulster Titanic Historical Society. John Parkinson, nonagenarian President of the society, is a sur-viving eye-witness of *Titanic.* The journal of UTS is *CQD Titanic,* a reference to the international maritime distress call (Come Quick Danger); in its difficulty *Titanic* switched signals and sent one of the first SOS (Save Our Souls) calls in history. And Belfast like the rest of the world has been happy enough to exploit *Titanic* for commercial reasons, or perhaps 'profitably commemorate' might be a kinder way of putting it. Belfast Special Dry Gin, for example, bears a *Titanic* logo. (I assume that 'it goes down smoothly' is not the intended message!) The Ulster Titanic Society sells *Titanic* tee-shirts, coloured prints, Society badges; the Ulster Folk and Transport Museum does a brisk trade in *Titanic* memorabilia, while a popular east Belfast restaurant, the Eastenders, has chosen a *Titanic* motif for its bar.

Finally, if courtesy of Simon & Schuster Young Books, children can now make a model *Titanic,* then in Northern Ireland they can be the beneficiaries of an impressive educational pack available from the Ulster Folk & Transport Museum, and assembled by Elizabeth McMinn, Head of History, Strathearn School, Belfast. One hopes it is widely taught. Certainly elsewhere, including North America, *Titanic* has become a favourite classroom project, at once manageable and diverse, local and international, a richly researched subject in which pupils can submerse themselves, but a subject still open-ended and provocative with yet unanswered questions.

A Ship of State

In order to stimulate pupil curiosity, the Northern Ireland educational pack rightly addresses the kinds of questions posed by the American and British official inquiries, as well as the mystery of the *Californian,* which heightened both the dramatic and the otherworldly dimensions of the tragedy. What it does not address, understandably, is what is nearer at hand - the social, sectarian, and political surround of the building of *Titanic.* The historian Jonathan Bardon writes that 'On the very day people in Belfast were reading the first terrible details of the loss of the *Titanic,* the first important vote on the Third Irish Home Rule Bill had been taken amidst angry scenes in the House of Commons. It was a moment long awaited by the Nationalists of the Irish Party and long feared by the Unionists'. It was in 1912, five months after the loss of *Titanic,* that tens of thousands of loyalists signed a Covenant pledging opposition to Home Rule for Ireland and their consequent ejection from the United Kingdom.

Unionists (those opposed to Home Rule) were buoyed and emboldened in the North partly by their industrial strength and pride. Almost three months after the loss of *Titanic* (mid-July), during what seems in retrospect a dangerous summer, a special report in *Engineering* magazine, 'Harland and Wolff's Works at Belfast', began:

> Public interest in Ireland is at the moment associated chiefly with political questions, and particularly with the attitude of Ulster towards the Home Rule scheme; but the members of the Institution of Mechanical Engineers, when they visit Belfast at the end of this month, will find little outward evidence of the trouble which agitates the keen politician. They will, instead, have forced upon their notice the undoubted fact that, from the industrial point of view, Belfast is very prosperous; it probably was never more so, especially as regards shipbuilding and engineering.

This long, carefully researched and richly illustrated report is *Hamlet* without the Prince: astonishingly, *Titanic* is merely alluded to in the brief history of the Yard in the sentence: 'and then a great step was made in 1911, when there were completed two more ships of the Olympic type, with a tonnage of over 45,000 tons'. Either the report was conceived and largely written before the disaster (with the opening paragraph prefixed later) or it was researched courtesy of Harland & Wolff on condition that the Yard's most famous ship would remain unnamed. One way or another, the impressions given are that the loss of *Titanic* was of no industrial or financial consequence to Belfast, and that politics and shipbuilding were a twain of no convergence. The waters had closed over her whilst life, work and profits had resumed as far as the vested interests were concerned. The vanity of human wishes!

But there is such a thing as the collective psychology of a people or community, and political stress can damage the collective psyche. Over time, as reaction to the loss (Southampton and Belfast were cities 'destroyed' by the news) gave way to constitutional tension and defiance in Ulster, then to the Great War, then to Easter 1916, then to the post-War 'Troubles', *Titanic* took its place among the shocks administered to once secure Britons who had now to think of themselves as loyalists and to double-plate their insecurity with steel.

With two cataclysmic (if unequal) historical events, the Great War and the foundering of *Titanic*, Ulster people have identified intimately. Both events have supplied much of the sunken furniture of the collective Ulster mind. It would be untrue to say that it has been exclusively a unionist identification (that is, an identification on the part of those in the province who see themselves as British), but it has been largely the case. What is interesting is that whereas the modern unionist consciousness was forged in the 1880s (in the defining opposition to English Liberal and Irish Nationalist plans for Home Rule), only thirty years later those doughty opponents identified with astounding losses and disasters (*Titanic* and the Somme and other Great War reversals), seeming to keep Home Rule at bay, as it were, largely by historical default.

It may be that there are certain setbacks of such magnitude and heroism (in this case the vicarious heroism of many of the passengers and crew of *Titanic,* and the retrospective sense of the heroic intensity of local labour that went into the ship) that they serve to sustain and temper a people, instead of weakening them; or else, perhaps, the setbacks come to have an energising emblematic power. (One thinks of the importance of 1798, the Famine, and Easter 1916 for Irish nationalists.) But it may also be that like the Somme, the loss of *Titanic* has come to symbolise unconsciously the thwarted nationhood of Ulster Protestants. Perhaps at the level of community dreamwork, the foundering of the ship and the founding of Northern Ireland were intertwined; the ship *became* Northern Ireland. This was a statelet that invited the pride in which it was fashioned – both the splendidly arrogant Stormont Parliament buildings and the splendidly reassuring burgher palace, Belfast City Hall, could be seen as figurative and stationary *Titanic*s – but it was always in danger of being sunk by the chillingly impersonal 'iceberg dynamics' of Irish nationalism.

The catastrophe proved to be more than a shock. Rather was it a collective trauma, the effects of which were passed from the generation of 1912 to the two succeeding generations. It had been a specific wound but over time it became a community disturbance. Of course, there remained in the people of east Belfast great pride in this favourite among the leviathans they had, as it were, fostered, fitted out and launched upon the world to seek their fortune. But the pride was severely dented or torn by the brute fact of the early peacetime sinking, which in maritime terms meant failure that annulled the imaginary success. Meanwhile, the civil commotions that followed 1912, and amidst which Northern Ireland (contemporary Ulster) was itself launched in 1921, caused the *Titanic* disaster to be in the short term negatively implicated in political instabilities and inequalities. Northern Ireland seemed itself to be a newly launched ship of state that felt compelled to use its own bulkhead system of social differentiation and discrimination between unionists and nationalists, Protestants and Catholics, in order to maintain its seaworthiness. (The bulkheads proved not to be high enough, after all, either in the ship or in the state.) The fact and fate of *Titanic* could hardly be contemplated with equanimity: the Ulster perspectives on them were too radically different. For sixty years or so the fact and fate were effectively denied.

Meanwhile, there have certainly been nationalists who rejected the emotional appeal of the *Titanic* story. I doubt if they have done so chiefly because of the 113 third-class passengers the ship picked up on its last stop, Queenstown (Cobh). Most of these were Irish emigrants on their way to America, two-thirds of whom perished. But *Titanic* was not primarily an emigrant ship and it was hardly comparable to the 'coffin ships' of the previous century during the Famine years; besides, loss of life was sadly international. Rather, the reason for rejection was ideological; the quarrel was with Ulster Protestants – of whom the Harland & Wolff shipyard was predominantly made up – rather than English policy-makers in Ireland. Nationalists saw Orange *hubris* where American blacks saw white *hubris*; behind both were alleged injustice and mistreatment. And in the sinking, blacks and nationalists saw Nemesis at work. Here was a third version of The Race Question (this one called at the time The Irish Question) raised by *Titanic*.

Yet my hunch is that Ulster nationalist reaction against the appeal of the *Titanic* disaster was strongest after the creation of Northern Ireland in 1921. Certainly Fr Browne read no troubling political significance into the tragedy. At John Redmond's request, 80,000 men of the Irish Volunteers (a nationalist militia) volunteered for the British Army in the Great War. The Irish religious orders were asked to supply chaplains and Fr Browne joined the Irish Guards in 1916; he went to the Front in France and Flanders and stayed there until the end of the war. He was five times a casualty and was gassed; he was awarded the Military Cross. His commanding officer, Colonel (later Field-Marshal Earl) Alexander – an Ulsterman of Scots stock – called him 'the bravest man I ever met' and remained a lifelong friend. A year after the war Fr Browne met Rudyard Kipling, whose Irish Guardsman son was killed in the war. Kipling (whom Browne photographed) was fervently pro-Unionist but this was no impediment to cordiality and the writer pays tribute to the chaplain in his account of the Irish Guards in the Great War.

It was, I suspect, after partition that anti-*Titanic* sentiment arose among Irish nationalists and even Irish Catholics, when politics had soured relations on the island. In any case, a friend tells me that at his National school in Tipperary in the 1950s, the loss of *Titanic* was explained to him by a teacher as retribution for loyalist bigotry. This would have been the sectarian backlash to overweening loyalist pride in the ships that Belfast built: 'If Britain rules the waves, Belfast builds the ships' was the boast I heard in the city when a boy. And the inequality of British society, of which *Titanic* was said to be a floating example, found its equivalent, perhaps, in the inequality of post-partition

Ulster society. My friend also tells me that the same teacher explained how the registration number of *Titanic,* if held up to a mirror, revealed the slogan 'No Pope'! (in fact, No. 401 was the work order number of the ship, but perhaps another number was involved somewhere down the assembly line.) Anthony Cronin's long 1931 poem, 'R.M.S. Titanic' has some very impressive lines, often in the manner of W. H. Auden. But by omission Cronin has a sectarian and racial take on the disaster. He manages oddly to turn *Titanic* into primarily a vindictive act against the oppressed rural Irish and dismisses Belfast in three lines:

> And they will bless the Pope this time in building
> It in a Belfast of exorbitant virtue
> Bound still by decent business's iron tramlines.

But in fact, Ulster's fundamentalist Protestants (whose faith at the time far outweighed their sense of national identity) also saw the retributive hand of God in the sinking. Indeed, they continue to do so. A short time ago a knowledgeable little tract by Robert E. Surgenor, an evangelist, was delivered to my home in Belfast entitled 'The Titanic'. In it, the life and death of the ship illustrates biblical warnings and lessons, including Proverbs 27:1 ('Boast not thyself of to morrow; for thou knowest not what a day may bring forth') and Job 9:26 ('They are passed away as the swift ships: as the eagle that hasteth to the prey'). 'Unlike the Titanic', the tract says, 'God has a Lifeboat for all, and that Lifeboat is Christ!' Distribution of the tract originated in Lurgan, Co. Armagh. The *Titanic* sinking dramatically re-activated the Christian Lifeboat metaphor, as we have noted, yet the hymn-singing aboard the sinking vessel connects the

tragedy more specifically with Protestant hymnody and sal-
vationism and thereby returns the ship to its origin, one of
the more evangelical corners of the world.

We could be forgiven for thinking that the collective attitude of denial regarding *Titanic* – and between 1921 and
1969, Northern Ireland, its government and loyal citizens
were in a chronic state of denial, in several senses of the
noun – changed only when the ship completed the voyage
from manufact to artifact, from industry to culture, from
the apparently discredited modernity of the ship to the cred-
itable post-modernity of heritage vessel and the post-industrialism of serious private sector merchandise. I will return
to this post-modernity, and its Ulster guises, in a moment.
But I want first to suggest that it was the conjunction of two
rather more specific events that has enabled Ulster people to
raise *Titanic* as a cultural issue.

One was the discovery of the ship's grave in 1985 by
Robert Ballard; this brought the ship to light in a way no
one could deny. The other was what in 1988 I called the
'New Realism' in Northern Ireland, whereby we decided in
cultural and academic circles to discuss openly and make
arguments publicly, uninhibited by a muzzling politeness.
Although this fresh attitude was to everyone's advantage (I
believe it spelled the beginning of the end for unchallenged
terrorist-driven politics in the province), it was largely insti-
gated by reaction against the Anglo-Irish Agreement, that
controversial treaty signed between the United Kingdom
and the Republic of Ireland the same year Ballard discovered the ghostly resting-place of the great ship.

Titanic had meant much to the opponents of the Third
Home Rule Bill for Ireland of 1912 – that Titanic year in
Ulster – and whose descendants massed in protest in Belfast

in 1985 as they themselves had done. The task of recovering pro-Union pride (not arrogance – more like the end of guilt – but certainly an element of defiant independence) includes recovering pride in *Titanic*, shipbuilding and other industrial accomplishments. This in my opinion will shake down benignly in the culture of Belfast, promoting equality by levelling the cultural playing field. Once come to terms with, *Titanic* can be accepted for celebration by everyone in Belfast as an achievement of the kind that made the city we live (or grew up) in.

Ulster Post-Modern?

Politics compose an important and obvious local context for the making and breaking of *Titanic*, but I want to introduce a different and less familiar (but still related) set of local meanings and try to weld them to the ship's international stature. For if there is a pattern to all that has gone before, it is the way the ship began as a triumph of modernity and after its foundering became, with some irony, a testament to post-modernity.

Even in Belfast, now a provincial and reduced British and Irish city, the *Titanic* complex today answers to the agreed features of post-modernism. What are some of those features? The existence of things only in representation, ideally in their commodified form as 'spectacle'. The transmutation of the thing into its image. The replication and reworking of what has gone before. The detachment of meaning from any firm reality. The absorption of high culture into mass commercial culture. Removal of the distinction between art and kitsch, high art and pop art. The replacement of aesthetic pleasure by simple fascination. The denial of history and historical patterns in favour of an eternal present. The substitution of surface for depth. Meaning sunk, splintered and scattered into the 'debris' of what was once unitary and stable. Some of these are cultural characteristics that Neville Wakefield in *Postmodernism: The Twilight of the Real* (1990) identifies from his reading of mainly French theoreticians that he associates with post-industrialism.

The sifting through of recovered items from the debris of *Titanic* in the pretence that we are reconstructing our culture and our history when in fact we are indulging in entertaining and commercial replication, is exemplary in this regard. Take, for example, the intention of a Japanese company to build a full-size replica of *Titanic*. The replica will not be a ship but a 'floating hotel' (the indictments made against the great liners at the time now made literally true!) and conference centre. It will be full-scale and follow the designs of Harland & Wolff's for the real thing, but there will be no engines or steering mechanism: the replication will be surface, the simulation only of what is directly visible. The cabins will be brought up to modern standards: i.e. 'none will be third-class'. There must be no echoes of steerage and poor emigrants. There will be, in other words, an illusion of democracy as a natural and widespread fact, whereas the replica will be host to the affluent and the reasonably affluent of the globe: the business elite and the moderately well-heeled tourists – reincarnations, in fact, of the first and second classes on board *Titanic*.

The plans for this replica are being drawn up by a Northern Ireland firm, Mivan Marine, which specialises in refitting cruise ships (the popularity of which reflects the growing leisure component of western society). The firm, which does much work in the Middle and Far East, has also proposed a half-scale *Titanic* for the River Lagan in Belfast: the disparity in scale between the Japanese and Belfast models would, of course, reflect the disparity in capitalist affluence between Japan and the UK. And whereas the Japanese simulation would generate serious money by being a tourist and corporate playground, the Belfast simulation would be a kind of provincial folk museum and work its passage in the so-called heritage industry, a favourite resort for post-manufacturing societies with only their own history to refit and offer for sale and recreation.

Yet a core of serious meaning has survived the profusion of *Titanic* images, associations, exploitations and representations. That meaning is human bewilderment and sense of loss; and it is human pride in leading-edge achievement that the *Titanic* calamity did not nullify but instead turned into nobility after the manner of tragedy. Post-modernity cannot happen without modernity, after all, and we ought, in order to set the historical record straight, return that modernity to the city in which our particular example was created – Belfast. Furthermore, to indulge in post-modern image-making is to short-circuit the longer process of reconciliation between the differing perspectives on Belfast held by the two communities.

A Neglected Modernity

The basic specifications of *Titanic* are startling. She was the height of an eleven-storey (high-rise) building, her rudder was the height of a house, her length a sixth of a mile. She housed the largest steam-engines ever built, before or since; three million rivets went into her hull. There are photographs by R. J. Welch of the ship under construction which show her scale by alarmingly dwarfing human figures. Fr Browne was astonished by the immensity of the ship when he cast eyes on her; from the first-class gangway he photographed the second-class gangway 'over one hundred and fifty yards away'. Combining the statistical superlatives of her dimensions with her innovations in technology and fittings, we see clearly that the *Titanic* was a remarkable product of modernity.[4] Not only was the ship, as Stephen Low claims, 'the space shuttle of the early 20th century', and, as Wade asserts, 'a wonder of 20th century technology', but because of the cultural meanings I've indicated, she was also a symbol of, as well as a product of, modernity.

In his recent book, *Making the Modern: Industry, Art, and Design in America* (1993), Terry Smith writes of the 'machine aesthetic', and *Titanic* and other Harland & Wolff ships are fine examples of what we might call the 'marine aesthetic'. Early Harland & Wolff ships, built in the 1860s, were known as 'ocean greyhounds', and *Oceanic* of 1899 was probably, in the words of the Northern Irish historian Jonathan Bardon, 'the most elegant vessel ever launched by Harland & Wolff'. Wade remarks the 'sheer aesthetic

---

4 The technology was of course – however advanced – of its time, not futuristic. In 1993 at the centennial meeting of the Society of Naval Architects and Marine Engineers in New York, naval architects presented their conclusion, having analysed steel samples from the ship recovered in 1987 and 1991, that 'brittle fracture', by which low-grade steel breaks violently when chilled, caused the ship to sink so quickly. The fault lay with the quality of contemporary steel. The search for causes of the rapid death of the ship has been a minor subsidiary of the *Titanic* industry (The Quick Sinking Question). A recent theory, offered in a BBC television documentary, *Explorers of the Titanic,* has it that an uncontrollable fire started in a coal bunker before the ship set sail, prompting Bruce Ismay to order a faster course with its disastrous consequences.

satisfaction' of *Titanic*. Hansen the novelist registers the effect of the first sight of the ship on one of his musician characters: 'Her name was right. The very sight of her vast shape – the cranes, the masts, the wires, and four enormous funnels – made David feel almost faint. The ship had a wonderful supernatural unity that made him think of music, of Bach, of sequences of notes extending and growing together into one vast structure'.

We could speak also of the sensory impact of parts of the ship (boilers, rudder, propeller, funnels) that we can register second-hand even in photographs. We can register it in reality as well, for outside the Ulster Folk Museum (Transport section) there is a Harland & Wolff propeller screw on display. In this case, reality is re-contextualised by the Museum in order to make a work of art: the screw is reminiscent of a Henry Moore sculpture; it is both machine part and work of art. But it is surely the case that the more skilled Yard-workers were not unimpressed aesthetically by the objects and material they were fashioning or manoeuvring and that by being so impressed they were living a daily life of intensified sensibility.

The visual imagery of modernity presented by photographs of *Titanic,* particularly those of the ship under construction, is also striking. The still photography most closely associated with *Titanic* is that of the Ulsterman Welch. Welch is thought of as a chiefly rural photographer, and his photographs as chiefly social documentation, aids to the social anthropology of the Irish countryside. But many of his photographs of Harland & Wolff shipyard, including those of *Titanic,* bear comparison with those of Ford automobile plants taken by Charles Sheeler in the 1920s and reproduced by Smith (who calls Sheeler 'the Raphael

The marine aesthetic: after propeller brackets

The marine aesthetic: arrangement of stern castings

of the Fords'). According to Smith, a certain iconography seems fundamental to the imagery of modernity: industry and workers; cities and crowds; products and consumers. Many of Welch's pictures of Belfast and Harland & Wolff offer such imagery with an iconographic gravity, including his celebrated photograph of workers leaving the Yard at the end of a shift, with the growing *Titanic* and *Olympic* receding in the distance behind them.

We seem to have airbrushed from our awareness the powerful images of modernity originating in Belfast by lazily permitting the superimposition of other images of the working and middle classes. To their enemies, the Ulster working and artisan classes are merely bigoted, the Ulster managerial class merely philistine. Here is the Irish writer Sean O'Faolain's critique of Belfast in 1940 in *An Irish Journey,* one that in its negativity goes far beyond the moribund Ulster Sabbath day I recall only too well:

> One felt that nothing could indeed have possibly come of that nineteenth century Sunday sleep, and the red factories and the grey buildings, and the ruthlessness with which the whole general rash of this stinking city was permitted to spread along the waters of the Lough but the bark of rifles and the hurtle of paving stones and the screams of opposing hates ... All the hates that blot the name of Ulster are germinated here. And what else could be germinated here but the revenges of the heart against its own brutalization ... There is no aristocracy – no culture – no grace – no leisure worthy of the name. It all boils down to mixed grills, double whiskies, dividends, movies, and these strolling, homeless, hate driven poor.

(Actually, in 1940 Belfast was helping directly through its industrial power to confront Nazism; O'Faolain's part of Ireland called that war 'the Emergency' and stayed neutral.) In O'Faolain's fevered outburst there are betrayed as narrow an idea of what constitutes culture as that which he imputes to Belfast, and an incapacity to look with curiosity at the work that filled the other days of the city's week.

Back around 1912, the work being done, the human effort being exerted, in Belfast was quite extraordinary. The quickest way to get some sense of it would be to get hold of the mid-summer 1911 Special Souvenir Number of *The Shipbuilder: The White Star Triple-Screw Atlantic Liners 'Olympic' and 'Titanic', 45,000 Tons, The Largest Steamships in the World*. This is a book-length technical and layman's guide to the ships, with plans, diagrams, photographs and statistics. For a further understanding of the work being done at Harland & Wolff, one could do worse that get a copy of 'Harland & Wolff's Works at Belfast', a lengthy feature spread over two numbers of *Engineering*, vol. 94 (1912). The immensity of the enterprise is what strikes. (Between 1907 and 1912 alone, 165,000 sq.ft. of shops were added to the already vast shipbuilding yards and 222,800 sq.ft. to the already vast machinery works.) The plates depicting various power stations, shops, berths, foundries, smithies, and gantries in this one shipyard are almost alarming. Workers are dwarfed in the photographs; they seem like tiny servants of the machines; it is unclear who is in charge, man or machine. Here are machines that make machines. The writer in the Souvenir Number of *The Shipbuilder* observes that 'Unlike many shipbuilding firms, Messrs, Harland & Wolff may be termed builders in the most complete sense of the word. As in the case of all the vessels built by them, not only have they constructed the hulls of the *Olympic* and *Titanic*, but also their propelling

Inhabiting the machine aesthetic:
electrically-driven pneumatic power station

machinery, while much of the outfit usually supplied by sub-contractors for ships built in other yards has been man-ufactured in their own works.'

This completeness of operation is all the more impressive in the light of what the writer in *Engineering* reminds his readers of: that 'It has always been a subject of surprise that works in the north of Ireland, which produce none of the raw materials for these industries, should take such a prominent place in production, not only in respect of the aggregate tonnage launched each year, but in the size of individual ships.' There is, apparently, received wisdom in the industry as to the reason. 'This, it is recognised, is the result of the enterprise, practical ability, and capable admin-istration of a succession of "captains of industry;" and at no time were those qualities, essential to success, displayed more fully than at present, so that the unprecedented pros-perity of Belfast marine industries is explained.'

And according to the writer, this captaincy consists in adherence to one paramount criterion, embraced by W. J.

Pirrie: 'Lord Pirrie, to whom must be credited a large measure of the firm's success in recent years, wrote that "merit
is becoming more and more the only determining factor in
life, so that to-day the invitation to the youth of the world
is, 'Go in and win'". The history of shipbuilding in Belfast,
from its inception to the present time, abundantly proves
this dictum'. Pirrie inherited the criterion from Sir Edward
Harland and the former himself rose from apprentice boiler-
maker to baronet and owner. (Like many of my contemporaries, I myself inherited the criterion from my engineering
forebears and it coincided – luckily for me – with the brief
age of 'meritocracy' in Great Britain – the age of the scholarship boy and girl – just after the Second World War.)

W. T. Stead, world-famous and campaigning journalist
(and spiritualist) who perished with the ship, is quoted on
Pirrie by the writer in *Engineering*: 'foresight, optimism,
incessant industry, the selection of able lieutenants (a sure
mark of superior ability), the constant introduction of new
and improved devices, and every possible combination of
mind and body, have been brought into requisition, united
with unique powers of organisation, to build up the greatest
business of the kind that has existed in the world since men
first began to go down to the sea in ships'. It is, though, the
acquisition and concentration of *power* in that age of trusts
and monopolies that nags when we contemplate Pirrie. As
Stead observed, Pirrie 'not only builds ships, but he owns
them, directs them, controls them on all the seas of all the
world'. It is one of the nagging impediments to an outright
celebration of *Titanic* and her predecessor and sister ships,
and the industry that built them.

*

There are other nagging questions. Even if modernity were happening in Harland & Wolff's, and in other cutting-edge factories and foundries in Belfast, were not the working class as cordoned off from it in their essential lives as steerage passengers on *Titanic* from second and first classes? Were they not simply exploited by capital, not co-creators but rather a lackey proletariat? And is not a positive take on Belfast modernity made impossible by the sectarianism that the city's industrialism involved; were shipyard workers not simply bigots? (Henry Patterson has analysed the anti-Catholic shipyard activism of 1920s Belfast in his book, *Class Conflict and Sectarianism*, 1980.)

Even sympathetic commentators have sometimes inadvertently encouraged a condescending view by presenting the workers as merely colourful, and the Yard as a folk arena peopled by quaint characters. But this is only a fraction of the whole story and a distortion when allowed to dominate our perception of what was going on in industrial Belfast in Victorian and Edwardian times. It may also be an unwitting translation by folklorists and writers of urban workers into the familiar, conservative and Romantic idiom of rural Ireland that has too often dominated disproportionately our understanding of thought and action in the island. It would be an honest supplement to the perception of shipyard workers as 'characters' to admit that many of them lived a hard life in the back streets of east Belfast deprived or ignorant of the finer things of life and that 'characters' are often two-dimensional human beings because their personalities have gone to seed. Whatever the truth of this, the shift seen leaving the Yard in Welch's photograph would in reality have had its rich complement of bigots, jokers, wife-beaters, right fellas, hard men, boozers, good husbands, 'desper'te' men, 'good-living' teetotallers.

But still, were the workers, as representative, modern, *machine-driven* as well as *machine-driving* man, not estranged and alienated from the modernity they were unwittingly advancing? Do they not indeed faintly resemble H. G. Wells' brutish underground-dwelling Morlocks who mechanically maintain the indolent Eloi above ground? Certainly they were physically dwarfed by their own collective end-product, and it may be that the humour and urban folklore for which the Yard was locally famous were generated to counter the estranging vastness of their successive productions with a sense of community that made metal and machine more human. Here is a passage from Wade, a quotation from an observer at the site of *Titanic's* construction; it is rather overblown (and curiously unattributed by Wade: who was this observer?), but may be no more than a verbal equivalent of the Welch photographs that capture the dismaying immensity of the ship:

> For months and months in that monstrous iron enclosure there was nothing that had the faintest likeness to a ship; only something that might have been the iron scaffolding for the naves of half-a-dozen cathedrals laid end to end . . . at last the skeleton within the scaffolding began to take shape, at the sight of which men held their breaths. It was the shape of a ship, a ship so monstrous and unthinkable that it towered there over the buildings and dwarfed the very mountains by the water . . . A rudder as big as a giant elm tree, bosses and bearings of propellers the size of windmills – everything was on a nightmare scale; and underneath the iron foundations of the cathedral floor men were laying, on concrete beds, pavements of oak and great cradles of timber and iron and sliding ways of pitch pine to support the bulk of the monster when she was moved,

every square inch of the pavement surface bearing a weight of more than two tons. Twenty tons of tallow were spread upon the ways, and hydraulic rams and triggers built and fixed against the bulk of the ship so that, when the moment came, the waters she was to conquer should thrust her finally from the earth.

Ulster humour is a form of diminishment, aimed at undermining the grand and the grandiose, and its 'locus classicus' was the factory floor. It is also a way of preserving the human in the face of the inhuman, whether it be the relative inhumanity of heavy industry or the genuine inhumanity of terrorism. Wells' Morlocks, like terrorists, are the very antithesis of humour and humanity. So if it is diminishing to regard industrial workers as urban peasants, it would be equally diminishing to see life in the Victorian and Edwardian Belfast shipyards as resembling that in the Ford automobile plants of the 1920s and 1930s that Terry Smith discusses – pure modernity without history, soulless assembly-line production, a 'regime' of modernity – with its Sociological Department seeking to create the ideal 'Ford Man'. Both 'Fordism' and O'Faolain's Wellsian picture of Belfast can be shouldered aside as inapplicable versions of Belfast industry in the time of *Titanic*, while we leave the modernity of industrial Belfast (certainly in the productive environments of engineering and shipbuilding) intact. It is possible, however, that the brief but deplorable phenomenon of anti-Catholic sectarianism associated with Harland & Wolff has understandably prevented us from properly appreciating the longer-term modernism being practised there.

That is not to say that this and other broader negative aspects of modernity, some of which I have already mentioned, cannot be fruitfully examined in the context of Belfast, that the wider cultural implications of such vessels as Harland & Wolff and other British shipyards were launching upon the world cannot be entertained from that perspective. For example, the philosopher and sociologist Jurgen Habermas has traced modernity back to the eighteenth-century Enlightenment and the proposed scientific domination of Nature (the *Titanic* project was popularly, even notoriously, regarded as trying to do just that – defy Nature – by ploughing heedlessly through the icefield), while the philosopher and sociologist Theodor Adorno argued that the logic of Enlightenment rationality is domination and oppression. This seems too highly charged a scenario for Belfast at the turn of the twentieth century, even in its anti-Catholic guise, but nevertheless, the city and its industrial and modernizing achievements are hardly beneath some sophisticated cultural analysis of the kind Smith devotes to 'Fordism'.

It might also be investigated how far the modernization of Ulster can be used to confirm locally the sociologist Max Weber's famous 'Protestant ethic' thesis linking modern capitalism to Calvinism, a thesis popularised by the historian R. L. Tawney and re-examined in *The Protestant Ethic and Modernization,* edited by S. N. Eisenstadt in 1968. There is an 1885 Welch photograph that might be a footnote to this: it is of a Trades Arch erected in Belfast city centre by the citizens of Belfast to honour the visit of the Prince of Wales. Models of a steam engine, loom, and ship adorn it, and around it appears as motto the biblical observation: 'Man Goeth Forth Unto His Work and to His Labour Until the Evening' (Psalm 104).

*

In the meantime, I was struck by Stephen Low's observation in *Titanica* that the sunken ship, lying on a flat, surprisingly fine-ribbed seabed (like exposed intertidal sand), has created a compact new ecosystem of fish and primitive animals. For I had thought, incongruously perhaps, of the shipyard that made her, as the centre of a *cultural* ecosystem, for which the Great Gantry around the growing ship might serve as metaphor.

It is true that the hierarchy of the British class system, reflected to some extent in the crew hierarchy, was also reflected to some extent in the workforce of the huge shipbuilding company that built the ship, running from management through draughtsmen and foremen to workmen and apprentices, with journeymen a kind of floating lower middle class. But this was necessary hierarchy, and social class and division of labour are not one and the same thing. Satisfaction of workmanship is a potent cement in cooperative enterprises.

Moreover, the pride in shipbuilding of Harland & Wolff magnitude was not just a pride shared by those fellow workers in the great industrial triangle formed by the ports, basins and drydocks of Liverpool, Belfast and Glasgow that dominated marine engineering for decades. It was not even just Protestant pride or unionist pride. It was also local pride, east Belfast pride. There was a network of family and kin within and across factories. The Yard was a complex way of life, a subculture, as David Hammond's documentary film and book, *Steelchest, Nail in the Boot & the Barking Dog* (1986), make clear. According to several historians, there was a working-class elite in Belfast, 'an aristocracy of labour', composed of highly skilled workers whose activities derived from day-time training and night-time education – all complicating the picture of an exploited, exploiting, benighted, bigoted working class. The Ulster Titanic Society tries to maintain this pride by commemorating (and celebrating) the anniversary, not of the ship's death but of its launch, not April 15th, 1912 but April 2nd, 1912.

According to Jean Cantlie Stewart, Harland & Wolff expanded in the eighteen nineties after Pirrie was made partner 'and began to acquire a reputation for strict discipline, above average pay for skilled workers and regional rather than national union agreements'. I leave the union issue aside, being interested here in the class of skilled workers. It was such an aristocracy of labour H. G. Wells had in mind when in *Anticipations* he predicted in the reformation of society the emergence of virtually a new class. He foresaw that 'the unorganised myriads that one can cover by the phrase "mechanics and engineers"' – not just 'the black-faced oily man one figures emerging from the engine-room' but the sanitary engineer, the mining engineer, the electrical engineer, the railway maker, the motor-builder – would over time 'tend to become the educated and adaptable class'. (He saw trade unionism as an unwelcome impediment to this welcome eventuality.) How far this has come to pass I leave for another time; for my point here is to disrupt the lazy notion that the shipyard workers who worked on *Titanic* were urban industrial versions of hewers of wood and drawers of water. Nothing could be further from the truth. And at the top of the local aristocracy of labour stood Thomas Andrews, engineer supreme.

The system at work in the Yard had its historical dimension, too. *Titanic* was built at the sharp point of a tradition of Belfast shipbuilding (the ship marginally improved on its own, fractionally elder twin, *Olympic)*, in a seaport with its own lengthy history, itself a conduit for a vigorous mercantile community. And feeding into that community were the advanced educational establishments of the city, themselves the product of progressive thought.[5] As William Gray tells us in *Science and Art in Belfast* (1904): 'the material prosperity of Belfast was the direct outcome of that intellectual activity that characterised the early years of the nineteenth century, when our chief educational institutions were founded, which were in advance of similar institutions in many of the chief cities of the United Kingdom. There is an obvious and direct connection between the educational results of the Royal Academical Institution and our chief shipbuilding yards and other important manufacturing establishments'.

In the light of this, it is clear that modernity was not a ruthless rupture with the past ('History is more or less bunk' – Henry Ford) but was pushed forward by innovation from an existing reality and absorbed past, not merely imposed from without and above by Pierpont Morgan, Ismay, or Lord Pirrie. In this, as in other cultural manifestations of modernism, 'punctuated equilibrium' (to borrow the biologist Stephen Jay Gould) is a more accurate description of progress than the usual 'radical disjunction' idea favoured by cultural theorists.

This modernism had, save in two lamentable respects – sectarianism (the mutual hostility of Catholic and Protestant) and the poverty of unskilled labourers in tiny houses – a benignly human face. Was Welch the photographer a paid promoter of capitalist industry, like Charles Sheeler, as well as a loving visual chronicler of country ways? We need a serious biography of him before being able to answer this question. But both were artists, recorders of modernity, and

5 *Engineering,* vol. 92 (1911) carries a lengthy and impressive feature on 'Belfast Municipal Technical Institute' (the 'Tech' in local parlance) that educated and liberated generations of the mechanically minded in Ulster.

Welch tempers the artistic and industrial hard edge of his shipyard representations with a humanity borrowed from his rural images.

Nor can the middle-class designers and builders be dismissed as uncultured Bounderbys (from Dickens' *Hard Times*). The career of Thomas Andrews, the Comber, Co. Down-born Chief Designer at Harland & Wolff during the era of *Titanic,* the master-builder of the ship, and who went down with her, is an apparently challenging case in point. The novelist Shan Bullock's 1912 biography is a 'labour of love', as Walter Lord remarks. (It is time for a new biography of Andrews.) Bullock is unapologetic in describing Andrews matter-of-factly as a good Unionist, capitalist, and imperialist. Yet this 'wonderful man', as Walter Lord calls him, was by all accounts an engineering genius and administrator *par excellence* (who moved frequently and at his ease among Yardworkers), working his way up the hierarchy like Pirrie, his relation and mentor, through all the chief shops and offices in Harland & Wolff. If anyone embodied a sympathetic continuity between the two realities depicted in the Welch photograph with which I began this book, it was Andrews.

By Matthew Arnold's standards this captain of industry was a bit of a philistine, but if so then we need to expand our idea of culture to accommodate him. On his Christmas card for 1910 he printed a sentence from John Ruskin: 'What we think, or what we know, or what we believe, is in the end of little consequence. The only thing of consequence is what we do.' I was pleased to read this in Bullock, for I had been simultaneously reading Ruskin on the role of iron in art and policy (in *The Two Paths: Being Lectures on Art and its Application to Decoration and Manufacture,* 1858–9) and thinking of my own engineering forebears.

I see Andrews standing at the junction of Victorian industriousness and 20th century modernity, and it is a pity that this man was prematurely lost. Recalling a visit to Andrews in Harland & Wolff, the Irish nationalist Erskine Childers (quoted by Bullock) wrote of him: 'His mind seemed to revel in its mastery, both of the details and of the *ensemble*, both of the technical and the human side of a great science, while restlessly seeking to enlarge its outlook, conquer new problems, and achieve an ever fresh perfection. Whether it was about the pitch of a propeller or the higher problems of design, speed, and mercantile competition, one felt the same grip and enthusiasm and above all perhaps, the same delight in frank self-revelation.'

This description makes a nonsense of the Two Cultures, both inside and outside Ireland. It is also, I believe, a portrait of someone who embodied an admirable modernity, unmatched elsewhere in Ireland before or after.

Thomas Andrews: master of the technical and human

AFTERWORD

M uch has happened in the world of *Titanic* since this book was published in 1997, though in the main, what has happened is accurately projected in *The Titanic Complex*, as the book was then entitled.

RMS Titanic Inc., salvors-in-possession of the wreck of the ship lying on the seabed, have mounted numerous and hugely successful 'artifact' exhibitions across the globe. Enough scattered lost belongings and miscellaneous items (that become 'artifacts' once brought to the surface) have been retrieved to stock several exhibitions simultaneously. The failed attempt to retrieve a section of the hull that I refer to in the book has now succeeded and this impressive recovery is now on display. The exhibitions are tasteful, moving, and respectful of the origins of the exhibits in what has been called a graveyard and memorial site. The original CEO of RMS Titanic Inc, George Tulloch, was disinclined to retrieve anything from inside the wreck itself but only from the debris field. He it was who had a reflection room as the exhibition's last gallery adorned with quotations from various poets and also myself, George taking as the motto of the reflection room my sentence in this book, 'We are all passengers on *Titanic*,' flatteringly attributed to 'Jack Foster, Irish philosopher'. George invited me down to the wreck but he and the corporation parted company before this could happen. Shareholders understandably wanted less poetry and more profitable return on their investments and so after George left, the company, using advanced submersible technology, entered the wreck and began bringing to the surface what the submersibles could retrieve. This generated heated controversy, pitting the wreck's discoverer, Robert Ballard (who regards the removal of items from inside the wreck as plunder) against the salvors and even museums. I have represented the arguments of both sides in my Penguin anthology, *Titanic* (1999). Since then, RMS Titanic Inc. has become Premier Exhibitions and returned to something closer to Tulloch's vision.

A different kind of exploitation, one just as moving for many, and just as commercial, was James Cameron's Hollywood movie, *Titanic* (1997). This kind of disaster blockbuster carries an invisible exclamation mark behind its title. Long on technical delight and accuracy, short on mature human interest and verisimilitude, 'James Cameron's *Titanic*' (and the possessive formula is its own kind of dramatic salvage-in-possession) was not only a commercial triumph but also a game-changing influence on *Titanic* commemoration, even in Belfast. Among other effects, it injected a larger dose of romantic love into the *Titanic* story than previous movies, to the extent that the romantic principals were assumed by many to be historical figures. (That there had been a real Jack Dawson on board the ship, whose grave in Halifax, Nova Scotia, is visited by young fans of the movie, gives a peculiar bonus force to the character played by Leonardo DiCaprio.) This romantic aura now surrounds all *Titanic* exhibitions and is encouraged by curators.

The ship itself still shares in that romance and this extends to a wish not only to replicate it but to resurrect it so that it can dramatically and romantically complete its maiden transatlantic voyage. The Japanese plan to build a second *Titanic* that I referred to in 1997 did not reach the gantry stage, but undaunted, an Australian multimillionare launched his own plans for *Titanic II* in Halifax in 2013; it is reported that the revenant ship is to be built in China. We await further developments, though such projects now seem to be vast examples of international urban and media folklore, with the announcement, moreover, satisfying the titanic urge without the need for fulfilling reality, in true post-modern fashion.[6]

Back home, *Titanic* is certainly now mentioned freely, in stark contrast to the embarrassed silence that reigned publicly in Northern Ireland for eight decades or so. Certainly, some of the talk is informed. The Ulster Titanic Society has become the Belfast Titanic Society and its journal, *CQD*, is packed with facts and reminiscences, new angles and corners of exploration. A good deal of research similarly went into the designing and stocking of Titanic Belfast, the huge 'Titanic-themed visitor attraction' that dominates what is hoped to be a genuinely vibrant Titanic Quarter of the city. Announced in 2005 (and opened in 2012), Titanic Belfast was conceived amidst the wake and wash of Cameron's

6 A convenient guide to the spectrum of *Titanic* representations is *The Titanic in Myth and Memory*, ed. Tim Bergfelder and Sarah Street (London: I. B. Tauris, 2004).

blockbuster, a movie that gave permission to everyone in Belfast to take part in the celebration and commemoration of RMS *Titanic*. (In the same year, 2005, the movie *The Lion, The Witch and the Wardrobe*, gave the citizens of Belfast permission to celebrate and commemorate the writer C. S. Lewis whom they had paid no attention until then.) Titanic Belfast has done wonders for Belfast tourism and it gets high ratings from visitors, despite the fact that there are few artifacts and it is a virtual and visual display: its contents are, as it were, the software counterpart to the hardware of RMS Titanic Inc.'s artefact exhibitions. Without a doubt, Titanic Belfast has rescued the *Titanic* phenomenon from its sectarian taint and this is a signal contribution. Naturally, *Titanic* is being marketed and there are market constraints on historical investigation and interpretation. As elsewhere throughout the western world, history is being translated into 'heritage' (a branch of tourism) which must achieve consensus of visitor acceptability even when divisions and conflict are being represented.[7] It is probably enough that Titanic Belfast has (like the ice-hockey played in the neighbouring Odyssey indoor rink) successfully transcended the age-old religious divisions of the city, while helping to put Belfast on the tourist map and make the city a serious destination port for the lucrative cruise-ships, many of which would dwarf *Titanic*. It is up to the local historians to distinguish history from heritage and, taking advantage

---

7 On this whole subject in the case of Belfast, see *Relaunching Titanic: Memory and Marketing in the New Belfast*, ed. William J.V. Neill, Michael Murray and Berna Grist. It includes an essay by James Alexander, CEO of Event Communications, the London firm that stocked Titanic Belfast.

of the good-will Titanic Belfast and other endeavours have generated in the matter of *Titanic*, to continue to explore this tremendous episode in Belfast, Ulster, Irish, and international history.[8]

Belfast, 2016

8 Two miscellaneous updates from 1997. The author quoted without acknowledgement by Wyn Craig Wade and whom I did not identify turned out to be the County-Antrim born writer Filson Young. Wade was quoting *Titanic* (1912) by Young, the first book published on the disaster that was on the shelves three weeks after the ship went down. I discuss this fine and prolific writer in my books, *Titanic* (1999) and *The Age of Titanic* (2002). Lastly: *Titanic* has fitfully inspired Northern Irish writers and artists, including playwrights. Three appeared in the centenary year of 2012: *The White Star of the North* by Rosemary Jenkinson, *Titanic* (scenes from the British Wreck Commissioners' Inquiry) by Owen McCafferty, and my own *A Better Boy* (a dramatic monologue delivered by Lord Pirrie). It is fair to say, though, that the Irish *Titanic* play has yet to be written, though the immense diversity of the phenomenon may daunt the would-be dramatist.

SELECT REFERENCES

Anon. 'The Loss of the Titanic' (editorial). *The Engineer 113*:
    April 19, 1912, 407–8.
Anon. 'Icebergs'. *The Engineer 113*: May 19, 1912, 511.
Anon. 'The 'Titanic' Enquiry'. *Engineering 93*: June 14, 1912,
    802–6; June 21, 847–50; 94: August 2, 150–3.
Anon. 'Harland and Wolff's Works at Belfast'. *Engineering 94*:
    July 5, 1912, 3–12: July 12, 38–50.
Anon. 'The Report of the 'Titanic' Inquiry'. *Engineering 94*:
    August 2, 1912, 161–2.
Abrahams, Roger. *Deep Down in the Jungle: Negro Narrative
    Folklore from the Streets of Philadelphia*. Chicago: Aldine,
    1970.
Bainbridge, Beryl. *Every Man for Himself*. New York: Carroll &
    Graf, 1996.
Bardon, Jonathan. *Belfast: An Illustrated History*. Belfast:
    Blackstaff, 1982.
Behe, George. *Titanic: Psychic Forewarnings of a Tragedy*.
    Wellingborough: Patrick Stephens, 1998.
Biel, Steven. *Down with the Old Canoe: A Cultural History of the
    Titanic Disaster*. New York: Morton, 1996.
Booth, General William. *In Darkest England and the Way Out*.
    London: Salvation Army, 1890.
Bown, Mark and Roger Simmons. *R.M.S. Titanic: A Portrait in
    Old Picture Postcards*. Loggerheads: Brampton Publications,
    1987.
Brown, Richard. *Voyage of the Iceberg: The Story of the Iceberg
    that Sank the Titanic*. Toronto: Lorimer, 1983.
Bullock, Shan. *Thomas Andrews, Shipbuilder*. Dublin: Maunsel,

1912. Pub. in U.S. as *A 'Titanic' Hero*. Baltimore: Norman, Remington, 1913.

Conrad, Joseph. 'Some Reflexions, Seamanlike and Otherwise, on the loss of the Titanic'. *The English Review* 11: 1912, 304–15.

Conrad, Joseph. 'Some Aspects of the Admirable Inquiry'. *The English Review* 11: 1912, 581–595.

Cronin, Anthony. 'R.M.S. Titanic', in *Longer Contemporary Poems*. Ed. David Wright. Harmondsworth: Penguin, 1966.

Enzensberger, Hans Magnus. *The Sinking of the Titanic. A Poem*. Trans. Author. Boston: Houghton Mifflin, 1980.

Ervine, St John. *The Ship: A Play in Three Acts*. New York: Macmillan. 1922.

Everett, Marshall. *Wreck and Sinking of the Titanic: The Ocean's Greatest Disaster*. L. H. Walter, 1912.

Forster, E. M. *Howards End*. London: Edward Arnold, 1910.

Foster, John Wilson. 'Imagining the *Titanic*', in *Returning to Ourselves*. Second Volume of Papers from the John Hewitt International Summer School. Ed. Eve Patten, Belfast: Lagan Press, 1995.

Gray, William. *Science and Art in Belfast*. Belfast: *The Northern Whig*, 1904.

Hansen, Erik Fosnes. *Psalm at Journey's End*. Trans. Joan Tate. New York: Farrar, Straus and Giroux, 1996.

Harvey, David. *The Condition of Postmodernity*. Oxford: Blackwell, 1989.

Hood, A. G. (ed). 'The White Star Liners 'Olympic' and 'Titanic''. *The Shipbuilder* 6: Souvenir Number. Midsummer, 1911.

Kern, Stephen. *The Culture of Time and Space 1880–1918*. Cambridge, Mass.: Harvard University Press, 1983.

King, James. *Virginia Woolf*. London: Hamish Hamilton, 1994.

Langenbucher, Wolfgang R. (ed). *Titanic* (Herbert Selpin). Gottingen: Herausgeber, Neue Filmkunst Walter Kirchner, 1963.

Lord, Walter. *A Night to Remember*. New York: Holt, Rinehart & Winston, 1955.

Marinetti, F. T. See 'F. T. Marinetti' in Dennis Poupard (ed.),

Twentieth-Century Literary Criticism 10. Detroit: Gale
Research, 1983, 308–26.

Marshall, Logan. *Sinking of the Titanic and Great Sea Disasters*.
Philadelphia: Winston, 1912.

O'Brien, Conor Cruise. *On the Eve of the Millennium*. CBC
Massey Lectures. Don Mills, Ont.: House of Anansi, 1994.

O'Donnell (SJ), E.E. *Father Browne: A Life in Pictures*. Dublin:
Wolfhound Press, 1994.

Platt, E. J. 'The Titanic', *Collected Poems*. (1935). Toronto:
Macmillan, 1958.

Shaw, George Bernard. 'The Titanic: Some Unmentioned Morals'.
Letters to the *Daily News* (with a reply by Arthur Conan
Doyle), repr. Bernard Shaw, *Agitations: Letters to the Press
1875–1950*. Ed. Dan H. Laurence and James Rambeau. New
York: Ungar, 1985.

Smith, Terry. *Making the Modern: Industry, Art and Design in
America*. Chicago: University of Chicago Press, 1993.

Stevenson, Randall. *Modernist Fiction: An Introduction*. Hemel
Hempstead: Harvester/Wheatsheaf, 1992.

Stewart, Jean Cantlie. *The Sea Our Heritage: British Maritime
Interests Past and Present*. Keith, Banffshire: Rowan, 1995.

Updike, John. 'It Was Sad: Our Endless Impulse to Raise the
Titanic'. *The New Yorker*. October 14, 1996.

Wade, Wyn Craig. *The Titanic: End of a Dream*. Harmondsworth:
Penguin, 1980.

Wakefield, Neville. *Postmodernism: The Twilight of the Real*.
London: Pluto Press, 1990.

Wells, H. G. *The Time Machine*. (1895). London: Pan, 1953.

Wells, H. G. *The Island of Doctor Moreau: A Variorum Text*. Ed.
Robert M. Philmus. Athens, Ga.: University of Georgia Press,
1993.

Wells, H. G. *Anticipations and Other Papers*. (1901). London:
Fisher Unwin, 1924.

Woolf, Virginia. *The Voyage Out*. London: Duckworth, 1915.